PRAISE FOR
SINK

"Thomas really does accomplish the extraordinary...[He] has constructed a sort of alchemy on the page, but one born of experience, from skill and from a trust about what will end up on the other side...perhaps one of the biggest boons of SINK is its insistence that care is, above all, shared. It is everyone's prerogative. In this way, Thomas has earned a deep bow."
—*New York Times Book Review*

"For the reader, third-person narration creates a buffer to a brutal coming of age, and perhaps allows Thomas enough distance from his trauma to bravely expose the vulnerability and resilience of his youth." —*Washington Post*

"[A] distressing, inventive, and often sublime memoir."
—*Philadelphia Inquirer*

"A crucial, incomparable act of creation and undefeated imagination." —*Booklist*

"Joseph Earl Thomas has created a narrative that reads like a request and loving demand. SINK is a new kind of memoir, remixing the best parts of the genre. Though cohesive, the chapters in SINK are brilliant and brilliantly different. Thomas uses the act and politics of oration to move us within the silences of desire. It's the way Thomas narrativizes encounters that makes this book different than any memoir I've read, but also so much more propellant than any memoir in recent years. It is criminal and absolutely delicious that SINK is a literary debut. It is stunning in its audacious goodness."

—Kiese Laymon, award-winning author of *Heavy*

"SINK is a singular memoir; all blood and nerve and near-unbearable beauty. A brilliant and fucking fearless debut."

—Carmen Maria Machado, award-winning author
of *In the Dream House*

"Joseph Earl Thomas's SINK is a powerful, moving, and artful testament to the sustaining powers of the imagination. This compelling coming-of-age memoir is often brutal but also loving; it's at turns critical, empathic, funny; it's searching and revelatory the whole way through. Joey is a narrator for the ages, a boy whose unforgettable story dares to expand the possibilities of Black male identity."   —Mitchell S. Jackson, award-winning author of *Survival Math*

"Joseph Earl Thomas has written an astonishing book. It's his debut, but he's already a master. Somehow SINK re-creates the state of childhood—its immense cruelty and immense promise. This book is for Joey, coming of age in northeast Philly in the late '90s: his video games and secret drawings, his longing, loneliness, and anger, his snakes and pet alligator and what happened, the roaches spilling out of the cereal box, the brutal trap of masculinity, the violence of family and smell of drugs through the door, every moment that lacked hope, every sweetness of imagination. Books like this remind us why we need books so much. With such tenderness, fury, and wisdom, SINK dreams a world beyond this one, shows us how to live there."   —Hilary Plum, author of *Hole Studies*

"I want this book for my younger self, to see the ideas and embodiments of Blackness and masculinity extended in these wonderful ways that allow space for nerdiness, nature, softness, and imagination with a rich interior life. This memoir has the power to keep shifting cultures and conversations into other worlds that are at first imagined, then made real. SINK is a visionary memoir."   —Steven Dunn, author of *Potted Meat*

"SINK is a book to read slowly and savor. With devastating, gorgeously wrought candor, Joseph Earl Thomas plumbs the depths of his childhood to understand how his family's ideas of masculinity and loneliness shaped him. Through it all, Thomas insists on a buoyant resilience, reminding us that with a tender-hearted fierceness, it is possible to stay afloat."
   —Kat Chow, author of *Seeing Ghosts*

"Written in third person, this memoir opens with physical abuse, drugs, and prostitution, three things that never abate...That'd be hard to take, if it weren't for author Joseph Earl Thomas's sparkling prose."   —*Washington Informer*

"Most impressive is [Thomas's] ability to write from the

mindset of 'Joey,' as he was called as a child. Thomas narrates the story with both childlike innocence and astuteness."

—*Sacramento Observer*

"In his debut, Thomas announces his unusual approach to memoir in the first sentence: written in third person and including both real and imagined characters...It takes rare courage to tell a story this harsh and unredeemed." —*Kirkus Reviews*

"[A] wrenching debut...Thomas's prose delivers an emotional gut punch...The result is a lyrical exploration of identity and survival." —*Publishers Weekly*

"A fearless debut that will change your life. I read this in one sitting and it moved me in ways I couldn't imagine. Thomas moves through brutal moments and uplifting ones with grace. It is a memoir that should be taught in writing classes from now until the end of time." —*Debutiful*

"Thomas tells his story through a series of related but disjointed sketches. In doing so, he creates a sense of disorientation, a fitting feeling for a book that highlights inexplicable violence and limited stability...Seeing—and feeling—the broken nature of the memoir adds an emotional impact to a story that had enough power in its simple facts." —*Spectrum Culture*

"Levity and warmth can be found throughout...SINK lays bare the trauma of a Black boy growing up in America."

—*PopMatters*

SINK

A MEMOIR

JOSEPH EARL THOMAS

GRAND
CENTRAL

New York Boston

Grand Central Publishing
Hachette Book Group
1290 Avenue of the Americas, New York, NY 10104
grandcentralpublishing.com
twitter.com/grandcentralpub

First Trade Edition: February 2024
Originally published in hardcover and ebook by Grand Central Publishing in February 2023.

Grand Central Publishing is a division of Hachette Book Group, Inc. The Grand Central Publishing name and logo is a trademark of Hachette Book Group, Inc.

The publisher is not responsible for websites (or their content) that are not owned by the publisher.

The Hachette Speakers Bureau provides a wide range of authors for speaking events. To find out more, go to www.hachettespeakersbureau.com or call (866) 376-6591.

Library of Congress Cataloging-in-Publication Data
Names: Thomas, Joseph Earl, author.
Title: Sink : a memoir / Joseph Earl Thomas.
Description: First Edition. | New York, NY : Grand Central Publishing, 2023.
Identifiers: LCCN 2022004492 | ISBN 9781538706176 (hardcover) | ISBN 9781538706190 (ebook)
Subjects: LCSH: Thomas, Joseph Earl. | Children of drug addicts--Biography. | Drug addicts--Family relationships--Biography. | Parenting--Biography.
Classification: LCC HV4999.C45 T496 2023 | DDC 372.37/4/eng/20220720--dcundefined
LC record available at https://lccn.loc.gov/2022004492

ISBNs:9781538706183 (trade pbk.), 9781538706190 (ebook)

Printed in the United States of America

LSC-C

10 9 8 7 6 5 4 3 2 1

Of all the protagonists in this story—both real and imagined—just Joey, the boy, owned an Easy-Bake Oven. Owned it the way his grandfather, Popop, owned sound, like the sound of Joey's name sliding out of smoke-black lips: "Joy!" he always said, "Joy! Come here!" Joey was timid, to put it nicely; and the Oven was purchased, with the help of Capital One, for his little sister, Mika, anyway. Joey had convinced Mika that she wanted one, and therefore, at seven, he received a gift that, through Popop's eyes, sat scandalous in the lap of his little black man in training. But Joey used it to make cheesecake, red velvet cupcakes, blackened salmon, fried chicken, and Chilean sea bass with dirty rice. The oven itself was tiny and pink, sitting on a fold-out dinner tray, flimsy and flower-patterned, purchased from the Dollar General just three blocks away. And beneath the Oven Joey kept a black notebook. No one ever checked under there. Knowing he would make mistakes, he wrote only in pencil and yet always struggled to come back and revise.

And he drew.

He drew stories of lonely sea monsters, moving pictures with tiny speech bubbles sprouting from their mouths like in comic books. Some of them had rotten teeth and smelled bad. They were very long and green like giant snakes and constantly angry. One such creature had a hood like a cobra because Joey had watched Steve Irwin play with one on *The Crocodile Hunter* and thought it would make a good pet. Watching the emotive white man in khaki from Australia made Joey wonder about different kinds of danger, about how some forms of fear were cool and quick and entertaining, and others were not. He imagined himself far away, like his sea creatures. Joey's sea creatures would say things like *gggrrrrrr, I'm gonna eat you* to humans rocking through waves on wooden boats. Then, without warning, the creatures would smash the poor humans' vessel into pieces. On the page, wood splintered in brown oil pastel shards through a deep blue sea of unknowing; the sailors aboard all drowned or woke up sopping wet on tiny islands with just a single palm tree. Joey had questions about why, if granted only one tree, it should always be a species without fruit, but this was ultimately fine, as artistically, it felt good. Stranded, the survivors would ask a scuttling crab, *Why? Why did this happen?*

"Scuttle" was among Joey's favorite words.

A survivor might, post scuttling around, stand there in a yellow raincoat, weeping under acidic droplets falling from an ever-darkening sky, shaded by Joey's godlike thumbs and the side of a sharp pencil. Starving, the survivor would watch sea creatures gorge themselves on the ocean's bounty, a contradiction to the brackish water Joey had seen in the Schuylkill if ever there was one. A sea monster would drag an orca from the water, sometimes a baby, and slam its body brain first on the rocky shore over and over again. The blood was gratuitous, thick in red marker to glisten wet, making the page feel so soggy and smell so good till it dried up and warped in brittle position. Upon seeing the bloody orca smashed into those rocks, a survivor might ask the sea creature why he did it. *Why slam them around like that, were they not dead enough?*

In the front of this same black book Joey wrote names in dark red lines, tracing over them several times each. First, middle, and last—no initials. He'd work himself into a fury, talking to these names in his own head. Overly simple dialogues, strange and unnecessary questions with no real answers, like those forced upon a child in real life, let's say: *Why you hold your wrist like that?*

Joey wanted these names, these people, to die. Or, he thought, *If people are going to die inevitably, young or old or in pain or otherwise, these people should jump the line.* Adults would find this cruel, but not as cruel as Joey found them. And he could never do the killing himself because, well, he was a coward, which never curtailed his devotion to such death in theory; he did not consider himself a super-villain. He would toe a careful line, somewhere between the kind of man that his mother, Keisha, might be afraid of and the kind that could protect her, if he ever, past seven, might be something more than both at the same time. So Joey scribbled the repeat offenders in blood. All the kids from Stearne Elementary school were in there. He wrote his grandfather Popop's name real small because he knew it would come up again and again; it took up so much space, so suffocating despite the fact that Popop also provided what little breathing room there was at all.

It was Robert Earl Sharpe, Robert Earl Sharpe, Robert Earl Sharpe several times smaller than nine-point font. To get the text so small, Joey had to sharpen the pencil against him, always. Up against the basement wall, hardly within his reach, Joey grinded the wood to precision. He had to stretch and scratch and shear his knuckles on the concrete to use the sharpener; each turn of the handle tore away some flesh, and so, the white keratin under Joey's skin hung open from cuts and gave the appearance that he'd fought back for once.

Joey, the Easy-Bake, and his sister, Mika, slept in the last room before the last room, a dining area of sorts, before a kitchen with the window to a forbidden backyard. Past them, in that rectangle of linoleum, was where Ganny and what she called her *real* oven lived. Joey watched Ganny walk back and forth from Popop's bedroom to the kitchen, bedroom to kitchen, as if those were the only places she could fit, like she might combust if left to her own devices in a living room or hallway. Before her hair turned all the way gray Ganny looked like Whitney Houston and wore a diamond-patterned purple silk scarf all the time. She chewed a lot, but she had few teeth, and there was never anything in her mouth. As a boy, Joey was always trying to look up in there, *nosey as hell*, she called him as he pried into her throat in search of something she might never say to him out loud. This, what he perceived as passivity—Ganny's hardly talking and automated work functions—frustrated Joey to no end. He considered that if she were only alive to bake the same nasty macaroni and cheese and do it with Popop despite the fact that no one, least of all her, got any pleasure from these things, then what was the point of living? The fruit of her labors—Popop's trademark rage—was always the same. Joey understood that sometimes, yes, Popop was angry at her for stealing money and pawning electronics to buy drugs, and so was he, but to Joey she was still better than his mother, Keisha, because at least she didn't smoke crack or do it with men for money in front of the kids. In this way, she earned the little of Joey's respect that few other adults ever could, even if he saw her as too much a cross between a punching bag and a robot. But Ganny was also a barrier between Popop and Joey; the old man would wear himself out on her and have little energy left for him. He felt guilty about this, head sagging off the top bunk and watching Ganny go back and forth. More often he tried to speak to her when she was crying and she'd just say, "Boy, if you don't shut the hell up!"

So he stayed silent on the top bunk, one lanky arm hanging over the guardrail when there was one, and often, he woke up on the floor after having wild dreams of racing through the sky like *Nights* on Sega Saturn or being swallowed up by whale sharks or tail-whipped by humpbacks working as a researcher for *National Geographic*.

Lying on his side, Joey could look out of two windows adjacent to said bunk bed and into an alleyway with a skimpy black table. The paint chipped and peeled and daddy longlegs spiders lived inside its hollow wooden base. He and his sister liked to imagine that the table was lacquered black from some ancient time long ago with substances no longer available to humans because the texture was so different from any furniture they knew. It was soft and flakey, but never splintered on their fingers or washed away in the rain; there was no telling how it survived for so long unattended. Without supervision Joey and Mika removed Joey's mattress and angled the whole thing down and out the window from the top bunk so that he and Mika slid or rolled down right out the window like Sonic and Tails into the cold Philadelphia air. Joey was always Sonic, of course, because Mika wasn't old enough to be player one until she could press the buttons on the Sega controller without stopping to look at them first. When Keisha came home with a brand-new baby named Julian, though, Mika got an upgrade to big sister and could sometimes play as Knuckles.

Joey couldn't understand why Keisha seemed excited about Julian; he and his sister barely saw her as it was, and the new baby was unusually ugly and frustrating. Wasn't there already not enough to eat? Enough anger at the kids already here? She sat the baby down and cats coming in and out of the window flocked to it, sniffing and licking. Joey and Mika saw the baby as an opportunity for experimentation. They heard those daddy longlegs couldn't bite, so they put the baby in the table base to test it; they figured shorter arms meant you could roll down the bed easier, so Mika rolled him and Joey caught him at the bottom; they were fascinated by how this ugly baby looked white and kept asking Keisha who the dad was, but she never said. The baby's future would be filled with forced participation in cardboard mazes, assisted flying backflips, bug tasting, grown-people clothes dress-up, and everything his mom and them either forgot or considered interesting. And he never did take to Joey and Mika's roughhousing, opting to watch from the floor, throwing a fit whenever he was forced into it.

Mika had all these butterfly barrettes in her hair, so whenever she climbed or slid or nodded it sounded like a whole bag of plastic toys dancing to life. The siblings would bang their heads on the concrete and giggle, knocking the lid off the table sometimes, and all the bugs would scurry out. That was how Mika first discovered those "alium" spiders. Joey loved his sister most in those moments—not just her cuteness, which he saw as being overvalued, but because she was his companion, and the only one who used the word "alium" to describe something other than himself. He did, on an honest appreciation of features, wield a noodle-like body and rather cartoonish peanut head that made him look like those silicon-based pseudo-real aliens from *The X-Files*, and such comments would have just been funny had he any confidence to draw from elsewhere. But he also had these buck teeth that made it hard to close his mouth. The whole thing was a mess. Because his mouth was always open, people would mistakenly think he was trying to speak, especially to some adult in public, earning him a pop upside the head. If a classmate saw, they bussed on his teeth until the tears drew disgust rather than amusement. So in a child's place, everything felt open and public. Whether inside the bedroom with no doors or out, the kids were always and never being watched.

But having no doors helped with the pee smell, a great relief to a bed wetter's domain in a place full of half stray cats named Angel and Bunny and Kitty Cakes or just Fuckin Cat. The odor wafted through one end, out the window to the yard, or into the living room that Joey could also see from his bed. Even groggy, he could tell which way was which because of that constant glow of green algae from the fish tank, the bubbling of its clogged filter and sucker fish puckering and slimy against the glass. In plotting his eventual escape from the apartment, he needed this light. He stared at the bedroom's light brown and flakey interior doors, plotting. They led to the bathroom, which was the butt-naked ass-whooping room, and the basement, respectively. Whenever Keisha was around, entry into the former normally opened with a sentence like: *Go get in the shower*, which made Joey feel dirty before, but never quite clean after. The pee got more sticky after the application of leather, for no crafty enforcer would use their hand to correct a bed-wetting problem. But then what to do with the belt? The family hardly threw anything away, so to the basement stockpile it went.

The other door in the kids' room led down to a mostly unfinished basement where Joey, after watching too much *Street*

Sharks and *Doug*, stashed a pet quail named Quaily that he bought for $12.99 from Birds, Birds, Birds pet shop on Frankford Avenue. Quaily was the cutest thing Joey had ever seen for $12.99, all black and brown and round and soft. Sharks, on the other hand, were too expensive, and he couldn't exactly cuddle them like the tiny bird. He was also terrified of the ocean, despite having great respect for the superior intellect— he said it just like that in real life, "superior intellect"—of cephalopods. Perhaps this was why he never drew sketches of Quaily, who was attainable, but wore out his obsession with the deepest, bluest sea on every blank page of his little black notebook.

Quaily lasted about a week before the denizens of 4444 Paul Street started to smell its festering body. Joey's own discovery happened while he was dry-humping his sister's big girlfriend Prudy atop a pile of damp clothes; they both froze in place at the smell. Joey sniffed his underarms quick to be sure the death wasn't coming from him either way. What a time for a dead quail. Joey was in the springtime of his youth, there and then, having finally embodied the poetics of dry humping— a little but not too much hip, catching the motion of Prudy's returning gyrations just so—when his previous love's death came wafting in from the side, horrifying and indignant. There was no way after this that Prudy, the girl Joey most certainly loved, who would grow to love him, too, as they grew older together, would ever agree to flee Frankford with him and start their own family in a place with no landlord and lower taxes. Prudy, a Seventh Day Adventist who was taller than

Mika and his aunt Tia but shorter and thicker than Joey and the high school girl across the street, turned her head to the odor, barely shifting her body on top of him. The slightness of her movement felt good. She always smelled good, too. And her real name was Violet, which, for some reason made Joey think her family had money, which explained why she always smelled good even though, on second thought, they most certainly did not have money. With one round and brown undimpled cheek pressed against Joey's face, Prudy sniffed around and spotted the bird body that he might have otherwise ignored in this circumstance, at least until he felt the tingling at the tip of his winkey and real life came rushing back to him all dull and pathetic.

"That's nasty," Prudy said. Then she got up off the basement floor, wiping chalky dust from her half-unbuttoned jeans.

This particular event happened either after the dryer finally broke for good or before the first time Joey realized it never worked to begin with. Quaily's death and Prudy's subsequent rejection prompted the first major reflection of this boy's life. He figured, oddly enough, that eight was a little late for such a serious psychological development. By five or six, plenty of other children who Joey was afraid of seemed to be more aware of their proximity to dead birds and sexual rejection. And since Prudy did not want to take the dry humping as far as Joey's aunt Tia, Popop's daughter, did, he deduced that Prudy must not have liked him at all. Ever. No matter how often she claimed otherwise. He cried about it because he was a crybaby and that's what crybabies did in 1996, especially now since he officially had no girlfriend *and* no quail and no mom and the whole legal guardian thing was iffy because he'd known forever that Popop was not a blood relative but Ganny's reluctant husband and he was hungry, like always, but Ganny was asleep and the Easy-Bake Oven broke down at times like this, looking suddenly like a little pink box with a weak light bulb that could hardly feed anyone. All night he would feel dumb, stomach growling and talking to the tapeworm he never really had, but everybody said he had, and he'd decided to call Earthworm Jim anyways. He couldn't wake Ganny to ask for things because she would get frustrated, which would make Popop angry, which would get someone hurt. Much like Sonic the Hedgehog, Joey just knew that life would be about navigating the machinery of other people's lust, greed, anger, or hurt, spinning signs and jumping high over the spikes, but not too high, skirting just under the sharp thingies on the ceiling, and most of all, being thankful that if all else failed, at least there was a roof.

Popop provided a roof. And there were so many kids who didn't even have that.

And Popop insisted on many things, but of them, two were most clear: that Joey had a tapeworm, and that he was definitely, and without room for question, a faggot. In fact, Joey could always expect to be called so more than his actual name. It wasn't long before the confusion about why this was so got taken into the boy's own skin and embodied as just another fact of life with anemic responsibilities to any evidence that might make something a fact. The women and girls, like Ganny, his aunt Tia, and Keisha, sometimes mutated the "faggot" to soften the blow, preferring Josephine or Sissy instead. He couldn't understand why people who were girls would bully him for "acting" like a girl. And their consonants, each time they spoke, weren't even pushed in as hard or held on to. But Popop was deep-throated, fast-talking, and repetitive. And ultimately, Popop was always right because he was *the only one in this fuckin house with a job.* It helped that he was bigger and stronger and Joey had heard, from sources most reliable, that he had stabbed some guy on gang business before, and since said alleged killing had been to this prison called Holmesburg that Joey would later discover was part of the All-American practice of experimenting on black and poor people and so much more. Like many of the people Joey knew who might have had things happen to their bodies, Popop refused to speak about it. He was a man with a job. And that job, after providing for somebody else's kids plus his own, did not involve explaining things to children. Popop worked at a metal coating factory down the block called Lustrik Corp. There, he made enough money to live under a mountain of debt, the intoxication of Kools and Colt 45, a white landlord looking half his age, and the roaches that were always falling, falling from the ceiling and into somebody's King Vitaman cereal or Oodles and Noodles. Joey considered the roaches particularly diabolical. What kind of creature was willing to give its entire life for the simple discomfort of another? Who were they even taking orders from? Or was the sweet sensation of what little sugar might be dredged up from the King Vitaman worth the sacrifice of one's life? For Joey, this was the kind of desperation that led to inevitable evil. The first time Joey and his sister ever went to the hospital was when a roach crawled into Mika's ear as she slept and tried to bite through her eardrum. After that, Joey was so paranoid that he slept with a blanket over his head every night. Then he'd dream he was being smothered and wake up gasping for air, his heart pounding out of his soaking wet Ninja Turtle pajamas. Both Popop and Keisha agreed that this was because Joey was so spoiled. If they could just stop spoiling him. For Mika's part, the roach made her more despondent.

Joey believed few things to be true, but of them, the most important would boil down into a simple equation: that all his family's problems were because Keisha and Ganny were addicted to crack + the fact that Popop was bad with money and a man, so needed to dominate other people like vampires need blood. Something like Crack + Angry Man = Problems. He'd miss that level of simplicity. Joey would learn soon that all any person ever wants is to dominate other people, just the range and shapes are different. It was all about how one molded that bruised clay of interpersonal relationships, how you might trick another body into subjection and hold it there however long, out of pleasure or obliviousness. Or worse, the desire to help. Intent hardly mattered. Popop might have known this from Holmesburg or Philly public schools or the streets thereafter, but he never got the tools or desire to articulate it. The man always seemed outwardly angry, or on the verge of anger, especially when he was laughing or smiling, and so Joey considered him proud and dumb in equal measure. Confident but infantile. Popop spoke really fast and stuttered a lot, which for some reason matched his box-shaped Jerry Curl, the front of his hairline pointing into a sharpened edge like a greasy cartoon devil. He even wore red leather and fishnet belly shirts.

Once, or only one time that Joey could recall, Popop walked in on Joey's naked body beneath one other naked body, that of Popop's very own daughter, Joey's aunt Tia. Whenever she was on top of him, Joey fake-closed his eyes, peering at her through the slits of his own long eyelashes. She was all cornrows and sweat and brown skin, with an upper lip that curled toward her nose just a little higher than most people's. Everyone said that she was a tomboy, called her boyish or a dyke or some combination of epithets but, to Joey, she just felt good. She was a rare manifestation of love and touch and gentle sliding against each other without the demand to know. In those moments with her, it was easy for Joey to forget shitty schoolkids or pops upside the head from Popop, the stale cereal and rude roaches, the need to heat up the water on the stove all winter; that mass of self-pity and anger, even at their apex, could sometimes be soothed by the simple, momentary condition, *at least there's this*. But things were all the more difficult the moment she was gone. Withdrawal. Popop walking in on them was the first time Joey consciously thought about the room having no doors. And they were on the bottom bunk, Mika's bed. Shame. But it was cleaner and quieter and not covered in plastic. This made it easier to hear and feel Popop over Tia's breath and the slippage between the two children's wet limbs.

"What the, what the fuck yall doin in here!?" Popop shouted, flailing his arms. He said this two or three times in the time span a normal person would have said it once. He slammed his hands on the top bunk. "Fuck type a nasty ass fuckin triflin shit is this? Tia, get the, get the fuck off that boy!"

In no great rush, Tia unstraddled Joey in silence, taking her blue jeans and tank top into the bathroom with her. Joey felt cold, as if Tia's skin and sweat had been the only things keeping him from remembering it was still winter, that it always seemed to be winter. He needed her, and he wanted her to need him, but she was a few years older, and it was becoming increasingly clear that she was not coming to need him in the same way. Popop punched Joey in the chest a few times with husky knuckles, the hands of toil, blackened from the kind of work he thought Joey should be doing instead of laying up under his daughter, hard and greasy.

"What the fuck wrong wit ya nasty ass?" Popop said, close to tears. It was the only time Joey could remember the man's voice breaking. "What you doin wit ya fuckin aunt? Ya family?"

Technically, they weren't really family. And Joey loved technicalities more than he did his own body. The story was that Joey's mother, Keisha, had dropped him off, and then his sister, and then his little brother, Julian, with Popop and Ganny pretty much right after she had them. Popop just happened to be the man that Ganny was with and sort of went with it. This was why Tia called them all little crack babies and BeyBey's kids. She used to say Keisha should really be named Brenda *cause that's who Tupac was really singin about.* Keisha was fourteen when she had Joey, and still dealing with her own shit: prison, crack addiction, abusive men, and johns she'd get stabby with for refusing to pay after a blow job in the front seat of their 2007 Audi A8s. And that stabbing would make Joey so proud. He and Keisha would laugh about it together as she denied it on her calls from the Philadelphia Corrections Center. He'd think about the man's blood pooling in the leather car seat and smile, wishing he could have seen it and that there was more blood and more dead bodies that would never be his mother's. But Popop knew all this protracted history and futures past and he still struck Joey, calling him a pissy sissy faggot punk on the bottom bunk of that room with no doors. He watched and waited for Joey to inhale and exhale, for the boy to expose his ribs, calculating which blows would best leave him breathless. Joey didn't know much. But sinking into himself, balled up in the corner, he certainly knew that Popop knew that he and Tia weren't *really* related and just a few years apart. Otherwise, Joey might have thought he was doing something wrong by reciprocating her touch so eagerly, for wanting to learn everything that just a few years' difference in another body could teach. Either way, he figured that midbeating was a bad time to present such an argument.

"You ungrateful. Little. Fucker," Popop said on the last few punches. And was he crying? "Where ya bitch mom at?

Better tell her come get her motherfuckin—" He stuttered on the *cu* sound "—come get her motherfuckin nasty ass kids." He paused before going on. "What you got to say for yaself? Huh?"

It was important, as a child, never to speak. Especially when someone asked you a question. It was not your place to reply. Questions were setups, staging elements wherein the reply demanded of you also justified the consequences of your reply. You just waited for the information to be beaten out of you. Joey couldn't speak in the moment anyway. *Don't fall for the question trick*, he thought. *Don't fall for it.* Sometimes when Popop was home, the boy's asthma would act up because of all the smoke, and the coughing might get him caught up if somebody grown thought he was exaggerating. He might get beat for making it up, just acting sad or hurt or confused, and then the beating would make him sad and hurt or confused. Or things could start with a beating and go the other way. It was a closed loop that rounded out smoothly in both directions. And Popop was smoke itself, vampiric sublimation. It loomed over the whole apartment, always watching and encroaching, and now, making it hard to see the fish tank and the sucker fish puckering out of Joey's one open eye. So he didn't speak, just like Gwen Stefani said in that video, and he was learning to speak less as he got older. It was a practice in being quiet, to think about what everyone else was thinking so he could anticipate what they might do and, if necessary, dodge it.

The Gwen Stefani video helped. Joey couldn't stop watching women on TV around then. They reminded him both of Tia and this girl Lauren who lived in a house down the block with her mom, next to the church. And sometimes it made him think of the high school girl with the big butt in the duplex across the street who was the tallest person in the neighborhood. Sometimes the video made him think of Prudy. Only one of them, though, Lauren, looked like Gwen Stefani and she was the smallest, youngest, and most boring, even if she was nice to Joey and lived in a house. He was especially not allowed to speak to her. But Joey figured he could love whichever one of them was willing to marry first. It frustrated the boy that no one else liked that No Doubt song, especially at school. They all said Joey was just a faggot who wanted to be white, so he gained practice keeping quiet about what he might like as well, until of course Tia admitted that she liked it too.

Silence was hard, though, because all the slightly older or meaner variants of children were in love with Jay-Z, shoving it down Joey's throat, blasting *Reasonable Doubt* all the time. Confusing. But Jay-Z, with all his strength and money and shorties and bitches and blunts and clothes and big grown man dick just made Joey feel weaker and more inferior. Jay-Z was completely unrelatable, and kind of scary. Jay-Z was Popop on a yacht with an expensive top hat and a pinkie ring. In the years to come Joey would try not to let slip how much he liked Destiny's Child or Dru Hill, but someone always found out. Tia would mimic Sisqo's "Unleash the Dragon," following Joey around the house singing, *You don't wanna see him unleash the faggot, unleash the faggot*. It terrified the boy to think of what Popop would do if he knew what he really thought, how he might actually feel, about anything.

Popop seemed sad and disappointed after hitting Joey. He always did, as if after a smack or pop, there was a sobering calm in the failure of Joey's masculine reformation. The man was unaware of how often his grandson zoned out into some other world. Popop, Joey thought, must have been disappointed with himself, with Joey, and with his daughter Tia, too. She came out of the bathroom with her clothes on and walked right past the angry man. Popop took some really deep breaths, relaxing the muscles around his eyes, around his mouth, digivolving back down into Agumon from Greymon, deflating in spirit as much as body. Joey wondered how many more times he could survive the transformation. Now, this was the expression he used with other parents and social workers. It was an expression that said he was not only willing but interested in dialogue, which was probably a lie but also true. He shook his head. Looking down, he mumbled to Joey, soft and weak, almost like he himself had once been a little boy.

"Fuck am I gonna do wit you?" he said. Then, he sat at the other end of the bottom bunk where Joey lay sobbing. "Listen, Joey. You need to go fuck around with one of them girls outside, one of Mika ol friends or somethin."

If only Popop knew. Joey was having a hard time breathing, but did manage to say, as he thought it was a profound defense of his entire existence, "Prudy don't even like me like that."

Got em, Joey thought. Popop would have to concede his anger now. The evidence was clear as day. Joey had asked Prudy, begged her even, to do the thing he did with his aunt and she said no. Several times. It was an open-and-shut case. It was not for lack of work ethic or desire on Joey's part, but a complete impossibility, as it took a certain sense of teamwork he was unable to achieve. He simply could not squeeze blood from a stone any more than Prudy's jeans over her thighs or any more wattage out of the Easy-Bake Oven so that the brownies would stop coming out all mushy.

All Popop said was "Whatever, lil bitch ass nigga. Ain't nobody tryna hear that punk ass little faggot shit."

Sometimes talking to Popop made Joey want to quit life altogether.

Nestled deep within Popop's logic, though, crusting up from the world of Man, lay the flaw in Joey's understanding. If neither his mother nor Ganny could say no to Popop—as there was speculation that Joey was actually Popop's son and not the seed of a pedophile named Tyrone—why would Joey think that Prudy should be able to say no to him? Joey had, after all, tried his best. Offered to *go* with Prudy and everything in between if she would simply do it with him. She grabbed his winkey sometimes, either so hard that it hurt or only over the top of his shorts; she unzipped her jeans but only put the tips of the boy's fingers in. Anything more than that was a solid no. She'd say she felt guilty because God was watching. This did not help Joey believe there was a God, especially not a benevolent one. And he thought, even more so, that people who believed in God, like his mom or her mom, or Popop, essentially everyone he knew, was just making excuses. Looking for a way to cover up things they did wrong or didn't understand. After a third or fourth time trying and failing to do it with Prudy, Joey felt so nasty he couldn't stand it anymore. Or himself. It was like walking through the kitchen barefoot listening to the squish and imagining what was stuck to the bottom of his bare feet. None of it was sayable. But Popop always said enough for everyone.

"And clean up that dumb ass bird shit in the basement," he went on. "Fuckin shit stink. Lil ungrateful ass nigga spend all ya grass cuttin money on these dumb ass animals that die anyway." As Popop walked away, his voice got lower but never took up less space. "I don't mean to yell at yall and shit I'm just so fuckin tired. Ain't nobody helpin me wit all this shit. Lazy ass bitch mom leave me wit all these kids." His light ramblings were inescapable. The sound of him was like those worm creatures in *Tremors*, always threatening to break through the surface, out of a wall. Popop was everywhere. The man grew legs or wings or fins just when Joey thought he was safe. "Little stupid ass bitch gotta deal wit these ungrateful ass kids all the time need to get some fuckin real jobs and pay some goddamn rent triflin ass lazy motherfuckin stupid ass bird in my basement…"

Joey mumbled something about how Quaily, even in death, had a higher IQ than Popop, reveling in the idea that no one else in the house knew what IQ stood for. Such mental pontifications made Joey feel a little too good. Hesitating, Joey grabbed a plastic Save-A-Lot bag from the kitchen closet and shook the roach eggs out. He wrapped it around his hand and went downstairs. He packaged up the dead Quaily, maggots and all. They drizzled on the floor in little plops and he could feel them whirring around inside the bag, too, on that sensitive part of his palm, the white part. Then he buried Quaily in the backyard that he wasn't technically allowed in, right in the same spot where he would later dig a pond for the alligator, as soon as he made enough money.

& THE
ALCHEMISTS GATE

A t least Joey knew resurrection wasn't completely out of the question. It just normally went wrong. You needed the right materials. All shit you could prolly buy at the corner store if you got there early enough: Water (35 L), Carbon (20 kg), Ammonia (4 L), Lime (1.5 kg), Phosphorus (800 g), Salt (250 g), Saltpeter (100 g), Sulfur (80 g), Fluorine (7.5 g), Iron (5 g), Silicon (3 g), and traces of other stuff. They already had a bunch of lime and other stuff in the basement anyway to undo the moist. But wouldn't putting all that toward a human body be a higher aspiration? A whole human body. Certainly, Joey could trust Ed and Alphonse Elric more than any public school teacher when it came to science. They didn't even know about *Fullmetal Alchemist* anyway; always so blind to the Truth. He and Mika could try first on Quaily, the bird, just like Father Cornello, and save the rest for Keisha or Ganny. Sure, Joey got popped a few times for drawing those sigils on the wall in color pencil, that "demonic shit," but transmutation takes practice.

Father Cornello was lyin anyway. He might as well have been working at the church down Paul Street. *Damn*, Joey thought. *Damn*. And Ed and Al didn't fare much better. A whole arm and a leg and a lost dad later with the same result. You couldn't call that thing they summoned from the Gate of Truth a human, let alone a mother. But still, they learned. Joey always wondered, thinking about Ed and Al, if all the pain was worth it. To get at the Truth? Did it make them better? Would it all be worth it in the end?

Back in 1996, when it used to snow still, Joey built an ice fortress to defend against his many enemies. Mika helped. A little, or as best she could, since she was still so little herself. Right up against the Post Office wall on the 4400 block of Paul Street was constructed a monument against humanity. There seemed to be no rush, as the snow fell all day and night forever, and in such a way that it was never exhausted by Joey's need to use it up. First, he shoveled as much of it as he could up against the orange-red bricks that shielded the Post Office. Mika followed behind him with snow cuffed in her hands, adding kid-sized lumps on top of the structure. A bulldozer came—courtesy of the state—and moved the rest of the powder up against the wall, but only on Post Office grounds. This was fine. It meant that, from here, Joey needed only to give form to the whiteness that was quickly becoming packed ice. He poked holes in it. He dug tunnels all through the mound and shaped sharp edges on the outside with a skull in the center, like a replica of Castle Grayskull. Mika got stuck inside some of the tunnels and had to be pulled out by one leg, and despite her near popsiclization, she kept laughing every time.

"This is serious," Joey said.

The view from the top of the fort expanded Joey's world. With fewer children willing to stay out in the cold for that long, the whole neighborhood became like a polar climate special on Animal Planet, all bare earth masked in cold, white powder, creatures beneath it wanting and waiting and growling and cuddling and warm, or completely unknowable. Joey considered then that he might stumble into a polar bear or maybe capture an arctic fox to love and to have and hold as a trained assassin, a rabies-laden guardian always tense around strangers but exceedingly loving toward him. He could domesticate and breed them even. Their tails would curl up like dogs and they'd want to snuggle all the time. He could name them Eevee, Vaporeon, and Flareon, respectively and in that order. Or a narwhal might pop up from a snow mound cracking open concrete and exposing the water beneath a dry ass city of trash and sewage and scum. There was definitely water if you went deep enough, somewhere down there. But there was also security in the blanket of white powder over everything. He couldn't even see the busted cars in the lot across the street or tell that the fence had barbed wire on it, everything uniform and in its right place and silent instead. The streets were full of rage, but felt empty. Snow would not stop falling.

"This is the best fort in human history," he told his little sister.

Mika, wearing checker-patterned oven mitts to keep warm and one of those big puffy jackets that make little kids look like marshmallows, stared up at him like he was insane. She looked bored tucking her cookware-covered hands in her jacket pockets and trying not to slide down off the top of the fort.

Joey went on. "This fort," he said, "is gonna protect us from bears and yetis." By which he really meant Ray and Darren and other neighborhood boys but also Popop and the adults in the house who he wished were actually just bears and yetis.

"Joey," Mika said, "I'm cold."

Joey had never seen a black person so blue. She looked almost like a Smurf and could hardly quit trembling enough to speak.

"You should go inside by the oven," Joey said. "Or else you gonna die."

And off his sister went, tumbling down the fort and waddling inside to warm up by the oven, leaving Joey alone outside, staring through the blizzard, dreaming to himself and unable to feel his hands or feet in the slightest. He could almost forget he had a body.

Joey woke up in the hospital. He wasn't sure it was a hospital at first since it was the first time he'd been placed in such a bed, but from the immediate cleanliness and warmth, he knew it was definitely not home. Outside the window he could hardly locate himself with all the snow, except for a single sign, "Max's," the cheesesteak place at Broad and Erie where he'd been dragged along by various adults so they could get drugs, believing that he, as a child, was unaware of the process. These were memories that, despite Joey's later-in-life vomiting of blue liquid and oiled animal on that corner after eating two feet of cow-bathed bread, fake cheese, and onions, smothered in salt pepper ketchup mayonnaise across the street from a gentleman's club after one angry black boy shot another angry black boy, he could never forget as a kind of origin story. Alone in his new room, he thought about the fort.

He figured that being in a clean, warm place like the hospital room would eventually mean he'd owe someone something, whereas the fort was all his. With any luck, it would stand strong the whole time and wait patiently for his return. It turned out his asthma was acting up, and nurses, one with blond hair who looked like Winry from *Fullmetal Alchemist*, came in to give him breathing treatments several times a day. He hated holding the machine to his mouth because the smoke felt dangerous, but he'd never gotten so much food and attention before. Three hot meals a day—none of which included Oodles and Noodles—was a certain kind of paradise. Joey spotted nary a roach during his stay, which also felt like a privilege he didn't deserve. He could sleep soundly, on his back even, with his eyes closed like he saw white kids fall asleep in movies after their mommies and daddies read them bedtime stories. Everything felt so unreal. And it made him guilty, so he lay there all night with a broken half smile on his face, waiting for something to go wrong.

Pneumonia. It didn't hurt. All he understood then was something about lungs and breathing. But when asked if he'd ever had trouble breathing like this before, at home, he kept lying and saying no. Pneumonia wasn't a real physical ailment to the boy, just a new word to keep him warm and clean and fed. He spelled it like "Namonia" for years, which also looked on paper more like a virus with a mind of its own that would talk to you and plot world domination rather than the dumb bacterium that caused Joey's lungs to swell but not burst. Joey thought a lot in the hospital about how none of the fictional characters he loved ever got sick, and neither did Popop. Perhaps because they didn't have time to inside the story they were telling themselves. Food distracted. Joey ate sausage and eggs for breakfast, beef stroganoff for lunch, and lasagna for dinner. His bed was lumpy, with thin white sheets, but the room was warmer than the inside of that fort or the apartment on Paul Street. Everything was clean and white. To the right of his bed was a spotless window where he watched the snow crush Erie Avenue all day and night.

When he wasn't looking outside or eating, Joey watched TV in the hospital room despite his suspicions that *The Cosby Show* was set up to convince him of something deeply nefarious, an alternate reality that hurt but was too hard to express. Winry and her friends kept checking on him, but they never complained about the shows he wanted to watch: Toonami mostly, *Cowboy Bebop* and *Outlaw Star*, *Zoids* and *Mobile*

29

Suit Gundam. They'd come back with a new friend each time, though, giggling and saying that he was cute but just so shy. *Why is he so afraid*, they said. The boy refused to answer most of their questions and was stuck on yes and no and asking for more food or to change the channel. They discussed getting a social worker to talk to him, but there was only one for the whole hospital and she was busy with the more serious cases. There were other children, Joey imagined, who'd been quite obviously beaten bloody or shot by their parents or legal guardians, of whom he knew there were plenty, and in this, he felt grateful that he didn't get punched in the face or shot at home, and equally grateful that he did not, in this particular moment, have to be home or talk to any social workers.

The nurses went on. *He's so cute*, they said. Every hour at the door, trying not to disturb him. Every hour.

After a while, Joey was weirded out by them. They were too carefree, and smiled a lot. They flashed all their teeth too much, and Joey knew that for other animals this was a threat, a promise. *They're like cartoon princesses*, he thought, *who might bite if provoked*. The boy wondered why they were being so nice to him. It was like they had a plan to bite eventually, just not right now. They would tenderize him into complacency first. Or maybe they wanted something from him. They would never say this up front, because the villain always waits until you have no means of escape to offer false choices. After they'd taken care of him, of course, they would *suggest* what he owed, what he needed to do, to pay. They might say he had to let them touch his winkey, maybe even all at once, because fair was fair, and they'd fed him for free. And he'd better use his winkey the right way or else they would just cook and eat him. He was doomed either way because even if he could do it right, he would get in trouble for touching white girls, and if he said no, they would hurt him or just be really mean and he would no longer have any food or a place to stay. He knew, deep down, that he would have to lick their coochies, and do it right, or they would get mad and threaten him. He didn't know which route to take and so he got quieter and quieter, which only made the nurses check up on him more.

But nothing ever happened. No one ever asked him for anything except to take his temperature. *Why then*, the boy thought, *are they being so nice to me?* If there were people living who wanted nothing in return, who bore no grudge against him for being a child, where were all of these people outside of the hospital? It made him more afraid to go back home.

The nurses, he then found, treated him like Steve Irwin finding a little lizard in the desert, doting over his completely regular body with infinite affection and pet names. *What a beaut!* they might as well have been saying. *Look at that pretty little boy there!* But then it occurred to Joey that there were parents who generally treated their children this way, and the contradiction just made him angry. He wanted to be an animal, wondered what it would be like to be a bat, a wolf, a snake, and for no one else's sake but his own, with pure and easy evolutionary drives that bred family only toward the intensification of survival.

On his sixth day at Saint Christopher's, Winry came in to talk while Joey was staring out at Erie Avenue, watching people, high and drunk, work their bodies around the ice.

"Hello, Joseph!" she said. "How are you feeling today?" She had the kind of enthusiasm that Joey imagined possible only in secretly mean cheerleaders. This made him like her less. And she looked straight through his face when she spoke, her brown eyes never meeting his own which, at their best, were burning holes in the linoleum floor. She asked again, "Are you okay, Joseph?"

"I'm okay," Joey said, practicing.

"Is there something interesting going on outside? No TV today?"

"I thought I saw my mom," he said.

"Well, maybe she's coming to see you, even in all the snow."

"Right."

"Well, if you keep feeling better," she said, "you might be able to go home soon!"

"Right," he said.

Before walking out, she asked Joey if he needed anything. It was such a simple question that it made him cry. He tried to hold it in at first, but his chest was too tight, forced in on itself from pneumonia and fear and loathing. He couldn't ask for anything real, but he couldn't let her see him crying either. In bed now, he turned away from her, covering his face.

"No," he said. "It's okay. But maybe ... " The boy hesitated. "Could I have extra dinner tonight?"

"Sure, Joseph. Of course. You have such a healthy appetite," she said. "You're gonna be back home and happy in no time."

This, Joey thought, would be unfortunate. To be sent home now or in the near future was a surprising kind of violence that he should have known to expect from a real-life Winry, but she'd surprised him with the suggestion, using her enthusiasm to try and trick him into believing, if only for a second, that it might be a good idea. *Naw*, he thought. *Never.* And then, in the hospital, Joey learned things about his body. At night when the lights went off and the nurses were asleep, Joey could play with his winkey in peace and discovered that this felt even better than when his aunt Tia put it in her mouth. He found that he could count his breath and think about whatever he wanted, slowly. He also discovered that, contrary to popular belief, he didn't even have a tapeworm. He was just growing too fast. His body stretched out in odd directions, nipple nubs came and went, little patches of hair appeared too early or too late and in the wrong places. They said he had Marfan syndrome, maybe, a heart murmur, and a big aorta.

"It would explain a lot," the doctor said, looking at Winry, "about his body."

But at home, such explanations were bound for failure. If Popop said he had a tapeworm and ate too much, then this little nigga had a tapeworm and ate too much, and consequently, would take that ass to bed hungry and without complaint. The older man's word was law, and law was, especially from Popop's lips, bad, almost unsayable, but it was still law, and it meant that there was no way out of it.

———————

On the seventh day, while questioning even within himself the potential biomedical explanations for what was wrong with him—no tapeworm but maybe Marfan syndrome—Joey got his first visitor. It was Popop, Robert Earl Sharpe, in the flesh and leather. Joey couldn't tell what came first, Popop or the pants and jacket that walked him in, glistening. The nurses all smiled at his grandfather, said that he and Joey looked alike. This reminded Joey of his uncle saying, "You know Earl fucked your mom before you was born, right?" Joey was brought back, in fact, to the exact moment his uncle said it. The man was standing on the front steps in a black tank top one summer, smoking a blunt. This claim was one of the few things Joey had no trouble believing, as his mother would have been a preteen then. Still, the boy was unwilling to give his uncle the satisfaction of a child's anger. *If they want me to react*, Joey thought, *they'll have to beat it out of me*. Thwarting people's desires this way, by refusing to react in the way they wanted him to, was deeply satisfying and exhausting all at once. Inside Joey boiled over. But the disappointment on his uncle's face that day was worth it. As if he needed the boy's upsetness to fill a void in his own confidence that would remain empty for eternity. Frustrated, Joey's uncle said, "You think you better than me or somethin, little nigga?" And yes, at that moment, despite everything he might not have been and never would be, Joey decided that he was damn well better than his uncle.

———————

If only he could feel this way about Earl. When Popop strolled into his hospital room, Joey wished he could walk away. What could he even say in the face of such overwhelming disappointment? And there was something different about him, about Popop, that made him immune to the simple manipulation that was easy with his uncle. He saw through everything, could make the boy's heart jump with just a grimace, and even if this didn't register on Joey's face, it certainly did in his bowels and that too-big aorta. Worse, though, was the jolly old time Popop was having with the nurses, them smiling and tapping his arm, him laughing and being so carefree, so flirty. Joey tried to hide his disgust, failing when he realized that Popop smelled like himself, clad in Kools and Colt 45; it was well aligned with a layer of sludge he left in the bathtub after his last shower—weeks ago—like a Grimer had squeezed up out of the drain and dried up there. And now the man was wearing a red-and-black leather jacket, red leather pants, dicked black Nikes, and a hat with a long white feather in it, as if they were different people in a different time and place. The multiverse come to make itself factual alongside a hospital bed.

"Look at you, curled up in bed like a little bitch," he said, standing over Joey after the nurses left. Then, Popop scratched his beard with those stale old fingers. Crumbs from his chin spilled out over the floor.

Joey didn't have anything manly to say, so he kept quiet. He was frozen stiff during Popop's visit, as if not moving would make him invisible, like he was the T. rex in *Jurassic Park*. "Tyrannosaurus," actually, was one of Joey's favorite words by then. But he was bitter because no one cared that he could spell it right; instead they just became annoyed as he slowly went through each sound. So he'd clip it off instead, saying *T. rex* with none of that polysyllabic satisfaction. He thought this, as if Popop wasn't newly standing over him.

"You glued to the TV here, too," the man went on. "That's all you do is TV and those damn games. Need to take ya ass outside more. That's why ya little punk ass got sick."

Joey hadn't even realized the TV was on. He was only looking at it to avoid looking at Popop. And then the mistake. The rationalization crawled out of Joey's throat in a whimper. "Actually, I was outside," he mumbled, still not making eye contact.

"Fuck you say, boy?" Popop sharpened his eyes. "You need to learn how to speak ya little ass up. You don't go outside enough, that's why ya dumb ass got sick, little smart ass mouth." His voice was just right, at that perfect pitch to make his anger clear but not alert the nurses waiting outside the room.

He kept on. Dumb ass got sick cause he didn't go outside enough. Boy need to get stronger. Need to fortify himself against the elements. Against the family. Against the chance that he might never leave.

"Peanut head ass shoulda at least wore a hat or somethin. So fuckin stupid."

Joey waited for Popop to leave in silence. Days passed

while he stood over the boy, berating him. When the man finally turned to walk out, Joey realized his fists were clenched under the blanket. He unfolded them, and blood returned to his fingers, slow and painful. A wave of tension slid down Joey's back, once slick but now getting more and more sticky. Those cilia down which the feelings trickled were growing weak, just like the ones pushing up the smog from his lungs. Pneumonia. Maybe the boy was sicker than he thought, and not just physically. Popop stood at the door, turning to finish Joey off.

"Need to hurry up and bring ya ass home. You don't even look sick no way. Left all them damn dishes in the damn sink, too. You ain't about to get outta cleanin," he said. "Better bring ya punk ass home and do some work. Stop tryna be slick."

Joey knew that the same dishes from when he left would be in the sink. There would be sopping food and rat poop, roach eggs and scrambled eggs, knives and maybe a screwdriver or two, some soggy frosty corn flakes from that box with Tony the Tiger's sickly cousin on it. There was work to be done. Big long work piled high in the sink, thick with grime and old grease, the kitchen floor still sticky like a cheap movie theatre and *God forbid*, Joey thought, someone else could change the fucking cat litter. By now there was a murder of cats at home, mostly feral and pregnant and always unfriendly. Popop kicked and cursed them all day, but he needed them there, to help with the mice. Joey wanted a dog. All these things he thought as the man spoke and he pretended to listen. *His throat must hurt*, Joey thought. *How do people talk this much and never bother thinking?*

By the time Popop had crossed the door's threshold, Joey was more tired than he'd ever been. Without having to force it this time, he dozed off.

That night he dreamed, again, of being someone else. He was playing *Street Fighter* with Mika first, Sega controllers in hand. He was Ken and she was Blanka. Then, before she could beat him—because she kept spamming that electric move over and over again—their physical bodies were training in some martial arts studio on top of a mountain with clean, thin air. The Eternal Dragon was there, floating around and minding their business. Joey and Mika rested their flat feet in the grass, and because it was a dream, the whole thing lacked insects and pain. In this great solitude, Joey taught his little sister how to shoot hadoukens from her hands. She was young, with tiny fingers unable to comprehend what around + punch meant, but she had potential. And in a rapidly aging and sparring montage, she grew taller and stronger than him, at which point Joey looked upon his work and saw that it was good. Mika was beating up men who were trying to touch her, challengers stepped up to get knocked down. One by one, then in droves, they stormed up the mountain with axes, scimitars, spells, and whips, but all of them met the same fate, screaming on the long fall down that steep cliff after Mika kicked and punched and threw them without breaking a sweat.

———

And there's another version of this story where Keisha came to stay every night with her Baby Boy Joey. In this version she becomes all the warmth that is not herself, is never spotted outside lurking around the building. For Joey, this is a hard sell; already, years of gaslighting and violence have turned his heart hard to her. The differences between her and Popop were becoming insignificant. To fix it, Joey imagines his mother as a child. When she was a girl, she tells him easily, it was her own father who first snuck into her bedroom at night. And by thirteen, she was already pregnant by one man and visiting another in prison before her water finally broke. Joey hardly understood what water breaking meant, he knew it had to do with the birth of a child to another child and more specifically, his own birth, and so it was bad without ambiguity. He pictured himself then, forcing his way out of Keisha's coochie or bursting through her stomach like an angry xenomorph. How strong and ugly they were. But why water? What was it about water, and even more so, how it could break, that was supposed to be related to a baby creature climbing out of a body? Whenever he asked, people just looked at him like he was strange, and so he kept trying to put together a sketch of his mother as a whole person, one who grew into the person she was now, whether she had a choice or not. Whether she chose to visit Popop in prison or not.

That next morning, Winry came in while Joey was eating breakfast in bed. Three whole Brown 'N Serve sausage links, scrambled eggs with cheese, grits, and toast with butter and jelly. Orange juice and water. He surprised himself, then felt guilty, after realizing he hadn't checked the grits for roach eggs and antennas.

"Good morning, Joseph! How are you feeling?" Winry asked. "If you feel okay today, you get to go home!"

"Not too good," Joey said. "I threw up a lot in the bathroom."

He thought the qualifier *a lot* made the lie stronger. He liked the word "qualifier" too, the way "Q" sounded at the beginnings of words, like "quail." Like poor dead Quaily in the basement, now buried stiff under all that snow in the yard. When the nurse didn't seem bothered by the vomiting, Joey volunteered that he had diarrhea, too. He couldn't really talk about his body to another person like that, so clearly and directly, so he said his poop was wet instead. He would cling to these lies as long as it took, the only thing separating his body from his home. Winry comforted him with a polite *aw* and said she would give him something for nausea, a word he didn't like at all because it described too many things. Joey kept eating his breakfast as Winry spoke, but, realizing that she might get suspicious at the way he was scarfing food, he slowed down. Maybe he should have trouble eating now, too.

After being healed and getting back home to Paul Street, Joey missed the hospital's safety, its privacy. *Why bother healing*, he thought, *just to step right back out into the world that caused the injury in the first place?* Like tossing your last Phoenix Down at the fallen and rising without a shred of new strategy. But, with a standard reluctance, he pressed continue yet again. Upon his return, Joey became obsessed with Popop's room because it embodied that kind of privacy and safety, absent the old man's presence, that might allow him to think and be different. It was the only room with a door, and it had a chain lock on the inside, so Popop could crack the door without ever unlatching it and look through like a crime show fugitive hiding out in a shoddy motel room. With each creak of the door smoke poured out into Joey's lungs, burning his eyes, shrouding the silhouette of Ganny or some woman reduced to an unrecognizable husk, lying wounded and musty in the fog. A bottle of clear Bacardi with the little bat picture in one hand, Popop would de-crust his beard with the other hand and say, "Fuck you want?"

Typically food. For himself, or for Mika, especially when her hunger pangs prevented Joey from playing Sonic the Hedgehog. Popop's hands were heavy, so Joey had long since learned to be careful with his words even though most of the time Popop just raised an open palm to see how the boy would react, happy with reproducing the fear, the squirming. Hunching down and away became a permanent part of the boy's posture. Sometimes Popop couldn't reach Joey through the door's crevice, though; this made Joey laugh harder than he should have, tempting Popop to open the door all the way. On occasion, he became angry enough to leave the room for something other than work. But only Ganny—her visage crumpled and sullen behind him—could have wanted that.

"We're hungry," Joey said.

Popop's eyes grew smaller, squinting, struggling to see if Joey had really said that shit. The man straightened his back, puffed out his hairy chest.

"Hungry? All that fucking food I buy in that freezer and you tellin me you hungry?" It was a favorite line of his, for both of them. More than Popop saying it, Joey was frustrated by the expectation that a nine-year-old should know how to thaw and cook red meat. How was he forever failing at things he was never taught to do? "Why don't you tell that bitch ya mom to get you some food?" Popop went on. "Tell that stank bitch to get a job. Where the fuck she at? And who the fuck you lookin at like that?"

Everyone knew Keisha's visits were sporadic, a random assortment of times where she would show up if she was kicked out of a boyfriend's house and had nowhere to go for a bit. By now it was an old joke that, for Joey, evoked neither hope nor frustration, but boredom.

Joey stared straight ahead, eyes not much higher than Popop's green-checkered boxer shorts, where Popop's winkey, like a big brown slug, hung just outside of a forever unbuttoned hole. Popop unlatched the door, then opened it just wide enough for a good slam. He mumbled ferociously, berating unknown demons until he'd worn himself out enough to say, "Aye, bitch, get up and get them fuckin kids some food." Even though "bitch," Joey had learned, was the common name for every woman, the boy could usually tell which "bitch" Popop was referring to by the man's tone. And the lack of reply confirmed it was Ganny. Most other women—though the end result was the same—would prolong the conversation, arguing Popop down until just before he got physical. Ganny, though, rose from the bed, slovenly and distressed in her nightgown, on loan to quell some other hunger. Being careful not to open the door too wide, she glanced down at Joey with disdain as she made her way toward the kitchen.

What frustrated Joey most was the obvious fact that Ganny would die young—with her always-and-forever-gray hair and sparse, prematurely orange-stained teeth—and there was absolutely nothing he could do about it. Watching her live a half-life under Popop's thumb didn't help. Joey always thought Ganny hated him for being dropped in her lap, for spending her almost golden years taking care of children who intensified Popop's rage with their unproductive and hungry mouths. *How much longer would his presence, and then Mika's, and then Julian's, require Ganny to stay with Popop?* Joey thought. So that someone would be home with the kids. *How much more did he make her suffer just by living there?* Thinking of Ganny made the boy want to disappear, to shrivel down and erase his whole big ass, hungry ass, useless ass self. He didn't treat Ganny much better than Popop did, either. No one did. He called her a crackhead and a thief whenever she stole something of his; he called her lazy and dumb as often as he could stomach it.

That he never called her a bitch, Joey would realize later, didn't matter. He had taken on Popop's worldview as a Man, had built himself up with the help of denouncing Ganny's humanity, and if Joey didn't understand the scowl she flashed back at him while lighting the stove that night, it would be all too clear in his memory. Joey wanted something from her that she probably had little capacity to give to anyone. And what could he give her? Nothing but a scowl right back—the gift, he felt, of repressing his true anger for her always stealing the only things he loved and her ability as an adult, no matter how bereft, to beat him on a whim, despite his protestations of right and wrong. So Joey watched her walking out of Popop's room and saw them both, himself through her eyes and all three of them then, despising each other with no hope of being extricated from their terrible cycle of dependency.

———

Popop's bedroom, and everything in it, was off-limits. Until the day it wasn't. Joey had cut school and tested the door, as he had plans for the bigger TV in there. And Popop hadn't bothered to lock it. Ganny was out—she never did drugs or johns in front of the kids, so sometimes she was gone for days— and maybe that was why Popop didn't lock it. He had no need to fear the vanishing of cash from jeans and leather jackets hanging by one long nail each on the four walls of his room. The children were supposed to be at school. But Joey hated everything about school: the nosey, underprepared teachers, their thoughtless lessons on the virtues of abstaining from drugs and little else. He abhorred the grimey niggas his age and older always anxious to test him. He detested the rusted metal fence surrounding the schoolyard within which netless basketball hoops hung above black asphalt where blood was too often spilled, too often his. He loathed the bright hopscotch chalk where little girls who knew him only as pissy boy would play during recess—everyone seemingly oblivious to all the world's repugnance and how they all got dumped right in the thick of it.

But on this first day of cutting school, he was free.

An older boy Popop had introduced Joey to—in the hopes of making Joey more manly—offered to come over with his PlayStation. Popop's every utterance to Joey always insisted on a more aggressive, less sensitive grandson. Popop's "be a man; stop actin like a lil bitch" campaign was the standing rebuttal to cold winter showers, the death of pets, lost fistfights, general depression, and every conceivable human emotion except for, but sometimes including, rage. Popop disapproved of Joey's only budding friendships with boys like Jeremy and Grant. They were too white for him, too scrawny, too close to his own age and therefore too meek, too gay to stand as proper influences. So when Popop introduced Joey to an older, bigger, blacker boy—the intention was clearer than anything the man could have said directly.

It was at Popop's job, Lustrik Corp., one day after school, in the same lot where Joey cut grass for twenty dollars every two weeks. He was in the middle of trying to bum five dollars off Popop—to which he'd usually relent after a few obscenities—for a cheesesteak, some snacks, and an Arizona Iced Tea, hopefully the rare raspberry flavor. Inside, rusty steel cranes grinded along the high ceiling, bathing metal bars and railings into rectangular pools of acid. The smell itched at the back of Joey's throat. There were piles of hard hats and masks lying around that no one wore. Tim—the high schooler who Joey first mistook for a man—was to be a proxy for Popop's will. He stood taller than Popop and wore a big book bag. "Weird, too" was all Joey remembered Popop and Tim's dad saying to one another while the two boys tried not to make eye contact under the dust and noise and cranes and that nose-hair-singeing smell of hot pooled acids.

Joey and Tim were nudged into each other and had to yell over the machinery, which was doubly strange for two boys who never learned to speak up or say anything with their chests. A forklift passed between them twice. They got across a mutual interest in video games, though, as well as what the kids at both their schools called white music. They even had a short laugh over it. Tim opened his book bag, its bulk made up mostly of CDs, and gave Joey an album from their mutual favorite band the Red Hot Chili Peppers called *One Hot Minute*. He didn't mention a return date. Joey listened to "My Friends" every day after school. It was the first song he ever memorized or sang out loud. In spite of his dislike of people and fear of speaking, coupled with the noise of a metal coating factory, talking to Tim was the easiest conversation he ever had. It was like speaking to himself or someone he'd always hoped to meet. But most of all, there was the joy of knowing Popop's plan would fail.

Joey never knew there were other black kids who liked the same things as him. Tim was obsessed with anime and video games, not real-life fighting like the kids at school. Popop would mock Joey endlessly for listening to that white-boy shit if he heard the Red Hot Chili Peppers album, but Tim appreciated it just as much, if not more. Nor did Tim call Joey a faggot for listening to TLC. Joey thought of their meeting at Popop's job when Tim suggested cutting school so they could play video games all day and how surprised he was that this suggestion came from a boy like Tim. He seemed even more meek than Joey or Jeremy or Grant, way too tame to cut school. Much taller and clearly overweight, Tim had a nappy head and laughably hefty glasses that got in the way of any other features. Joey saw himself in five years, though he prayed he would be more attractive. Or that grown women would think so.

Playing the game in Popop's room would be better because it was cleanest and the TV dwarfed the one in the living room. The privacy of the door also made Joey feel more grown up and safe. It was a room comprised of mostly bed, with the TV on a single black dresser at the foot of a king mattress. Next to the TV, there were three brown ashtrays littered with leftover roaches and filtered Kools cigarettes. An empty 40 oz of Olde English stood proudly in front of the cable box. Even with no one actively drinking or smoking, the air was thick with stale liquor and old smoke, which also clung to the walls and clothes and fabric and skin. But Joey had gotten used to the strain on his throat from the constant dry cough of being near Popop. The two boys moved clothes aside to make room for the PlayStation on the floor and Tim gamely offered to set it up. Joey fidgeted with excitement as the older boy pulled the bright white system from his JanSport, his hands sweating onto the bed covers. Tim closed the door before sitting next to the smaller boy, handing Joey the controller.

"Here, you can go first," Tim said. "I'll explain stuff to you."

The game was *Crash Bandicoot*. Suddenly, Joey was an Indiana Jones–esque bandicoot (an animal he hadn't previously known existed) sprinting through mazes, dodging traps, jumping over pitfalls, and collecting all the Wumpa Fruit his bandicoot heart desired. Joey was damn good. As he tended to be with all video games, but never in front of many people before Tim. With the older boy, it was easy to forget the most recent schoolyard stomping from that overaged elementary school kid just a few days prior, his mom's most recent jail stint, and even Popop's gun tucked in the ceiling tile just above their heads. For a moment, Joey stopped wanting to use it on himself or anyone else.

For the first time, Joey glimpsed into a future where being a nerdy black boy might turn out okay. As Tim explained how the game worked, his words drifted through the smaller boy's ears and across the room. He was focused, sustained by the 32-bit system, the comfort of an older brother he'd never had, and the infinite hours ahead of it all. Joey was lulled into an unfamiliar state of comfort from which he did not intend to return. And then they switched to *Castlevania: Symphony of the Night*. The slick and fluid movements of Dracula's only son from left to right, right to left, felt to Joey like finally holding his own life in his hands. Alucard's white hair swayed in the wind, slashing werewolves and zombies and a host of forsaken entities into pieces like butter. This was how anime samurai did it. Cleaving demons into fire and ash, their screams and howls flashing in the night, brightening the sky in this world and the next. Joey as Alucard, Alucard as Joey, chosen, finally, to do what he always knew in his body he needed to do. They needed to do.

Until Tim put his right hand on Joey's inner thigh.

And the boy's khakis seemed too thin. He hadn't realized how close they were sitting to each other before that moment: Shoulder to shoulder, Joey's legs dangling from the end of Popop's bed, Tim's huge butters planted firmly on the dark brown carpet. Tim's voice never changed. He never took his eyes off the screen. Joey's mind slowly backed out of the game. He fought it. Reality wasn't for him yet. The boy took a deep breath and considered pretending it never happened. Maybe Tim's hand slipped. Maybe he would just move it and say, *My bad*. In Joey's infinite disbelief, he even hoped to God or whoever else might be out there that Tim's hand on the thigh was a mistake. But it wasn't.

Tim moved his hand inward, insistently across Joey's pants, following the curve of his winkey with an open palm. Unmistakable. Joey dropped the controller and sprung from the bed, pushing out of Tim's reach.

"Yo, what you doin, man?" Joey said more than asked. The boy felt nasty, like he'd be permanently tarnished. His face would forever be the face of a little gay boy who cut school and invited another boy over to play with his winkey. Joey was terrified at the idea of what Popop might do if he ever found out, at what people might say about him that they had not already said, or that they might have the joy of being right about something. Had Joey done something to make Tim think they wanted the same thing? He couldn't think of anything. Tim wasn't forceful. He didn't make Joey submit, even though he so easily could have. But Tim's gentleness didn't make the boy feel any less like a half person. Joey's heart raced, yet he stood puffed out, working hard to appear tougher than he was. He needed to be the opposite of the weak, suspect gay boy that all external evidence suggested he was. Joey hated himself. He hated Tim. He wanted Tim to feel afraid like Popop made him feel, just in case. Joey was learning that sometimes fear was enough to mitigate greater conflict, to stomp out the inevitably more egregious violence before it happened. This is what he would come to think, for just a little too long.

"What do you mean?" Tim asked, in seemingly genuine confusion. Joey didn't know what to believe. Every lesson—and there were precious few—told him that gay boys—faggots, as Popop called them—were foul monsters who would fuck Joey in the ass till it ripped and bled unless he stopped being so soft. But Joey had never wanted to be friends with someone more. Tim wasn't a monster even if he touched Joey without his permission. He'd also stopped. But this was all too much. Too dangerous, an articulation of the in-between that was never given space.

Tim had to leave. Joey didn't want him or anyone else there. Not in Earl's room. Not anywhere in the apartment. Not with him. Joey had been brutalized enough as a suspected faggot in everyone's eyes—the closest sin to being a woman he'd known—and he'd be killed if Popop even considered that two boys might have touched in his room, reciprocated or not. Joey shrunk and fumbled with all manner of excuses before telling Tim to go. None of what the boy said seemed to matter, though, until he said that Popop was coming home early. No longer did Tim object. Packing away his PlayStation, Tim slung his book bag over one shoulder and walked out slowly, sad, but leaving. Joey wanted him to stay, but couldn't ratio-nalize it. Pride—either his or Popop's—wouldn't allow. After accepting his coming absence, Joey cried until Popop could get home and offer him "something to really cry about."

But Ganny got home first. By then Joey was sitting in

the living room playing *Altered Beast* on Sega. "Boy, what's wrong wit you?" Ganny asked, a little sour. She was tired and another one of her teeth was missing. Joey had always heard Popop's ramblings about Ganny trickin, going out and selling her body as a prostitute. He imagined that this was what she did when she was not around and that it had to be dangerous. He knew that she always stole things, like his video games, and took them to the pawn shop at Margaret and Orthodox next to the Fly Guys barbershop where he'd later beg the Puerto Rican guys working the counter to help rescue the very Sega he was playing while Ganny asked him what was wrong. He wanted to like Ganny so bad, if only for her asking, and the fact that she hardly ever had the strength to hit him.

Ganny never had a job, not one that Popop would respect because he would never allow her to have such a thing. In the state that Joey had always known her, a job might never have been possible. The boy had always pictured her in the front seat of a man's car sucking his winkey, even though he'd only seen Keisha doing that in the living room or the alleyway so far. He'd also seen those men punch or slap Keisha—one calculated time with force and meaning they'd devote to little else. He assumed it was because of some perceived inadequacy on her end, some slight that reduced the man's satisfaction a little.

Ganny's lumped face, and her new missing tooth, was then also the result of some perceived inadequacy. It was all Joey could think of when he looked at her. When Ganny asked what was wrong, the boy wanted to tell her. He wanted to know that there was someone he could side with. They had a shared enemy, didn't they? But he just couldn't trust her, thinking only about what she'd taken and denied, not what had been taken and denied to her. And Popop would find out everything in time. Eyes in the back of his head, he always said, ears in the walls. Confiding in Ganny might have given Joey some peace, but it wouldn't have made Popop happy. Conspiring against him, the skank and the little faggot, would only make their lives worse. Popop had informed them of who they were, until they embodied it themselves, repeating his work for him. So when Ganny asked Joey what was wrong—his eyes red from crying—he could barely be any kinder to her than usual. He said nothing.

She walked past him into the kitchen. On the plastic-covered loveseat, Joey fidgeted and died again and again in the game, transfiguring himself over and over into a werewolf, a gargoyle, a bear, a werewolf, a gargoyle, a bear, and wishing he could embody that kind of power in real life, that he had that sort of will. But he never passed the fifth stage. He almost went so far as to pray for the intervention of some deity. Ganny walked by him again and paused in front of the fish tank, its algae making her look radioactive.

"You sure ain't nothin wrong?" she asked.

Joey was amazed at how sweet she sounded, and how naive the assumption was that, if something was wrong, she might be able to do something about it. What she was doing only made the boy sadder, and the next time she stole his video games he'd ask, with all the world's rage, *How come you not asking me what's wrong now?*

"No. Just leave me alone," he said.

Ganny walked into Popop's room to wait on his return. Like every day he came through the front door fatigued, hands blackened and bearing gifts. The man had plastic bags in his palms, filled with huggie juices and potato chips. Joey and his sister would fight over the cheese curls. Then, upon examining another bag, they'd find water guns and other dollar-store oddities: cap guns and balloons, spinner tops, yoyos, jax, and plastic army men. The toys and the sugar kept the kids occupied and out of people's faces. Ganny didn't like when he brought things home, though, saying it would spoil them. And in response, Popop would grumble. The only thing breaking the routine this time must have been Joey's face. Standing at the door to help with the bags, there was something in it that Popop noticed, became suspicious of.

"Fuck wrong wit ya face? All frowned up like a little punk," Popop said, dropping the bags down on the living room table. Mika, only recently awakened from sleep, rushed to scramble through them.

Joey tried to adjust his face, to fix or contort it in some way, practicing the fake, closed-mouth smile he'd master later. "Nothin," the boy said.

"Fix ya damn face. Go back and play that stupid ass game or some shit. Get outta my face."

Joey sat back down on the couch. That he viewed Joey's only source of happiness—of learning—as stupid made the boy upset in ways he couldn't explain, not even to himself. Not long ago, Popop used to play those stupid games with him, mostly *Super Mario Bros.* He was really good too. He'd trash Joey's scores on Nintendo and talk all kinds of shit about it.

"Damn, Joey, you even tryin?" Popop would say, laughing. The man's Mario avatar sprinted across the 2-D plane, hurling fireballs at everything and always sliding down from the very top of the flag at the end. Five thousand points every time. Joey never questioned why they played that first level so much though, over and over again. Repetition made it thoughtless and inevitable after a while but still, it was a rare time when they both smiled together. Joey's hands were too small, his coordination too weak to be serious competition, but the boy always had fun, win or lose. Some of his fondest memories are losing through those first few levels. Popop was a great whistler, and he'd match the theme song while trouncing the boy time and again. Joey made fun of him for looking down at the buttons on the controller and back at the screen and moving his real-life body with the character how old people do. Joey can still see the smirk on Popop's face when Mario jumps from the top of a brick pile and slips all the way down that flag. "I'm bussin that ass, cutty," he'd say.

Joey liked that as he got older, the video games grew more complex. His coordination got better, and JRPGs eventually taught him to read. Popop hung back and drank and smoked more, caroused, and yelled at times. The boy and the man grew apart, and by the time Joey was eight or nine, they were practically estranged. On this particular day, when Joey had cut school with Tim, he was glad for the rift that had grown between them. Even happier that the man hadn't found out about Tim. Popop accepted Joey's nothing excuse and went into his room with no noise to pour a glass of Bacardi. He really was in a good mood. He didn't even close the door. Mika sat behind Joey to watch him play the game, and the boy blew into the *Sonic & Knuckles* Sega cartridge to get the dust and cockroach eggs out. He was excited to play, thinking to himself that Popop would never know what happened.

Until the phone rang.

Few people called the house: bill collectors, Popop's mom, somebody from jail, or social services. Popop seemed calm and collected as he grabbed the rotary. He leaned against the wall, watching Joey watch him. The boy's heart beat too fast, wishing he could hear what the other person on the line was saying. Popop's tone was between even and joyful; it was undeniably the voice he used to talk to strangers or white people about the kids. And while his tone didn't change, he frowned and squinched his face up more as the conversation went on.

"Uh-huh," he said. "Yes. Oh, is that so? Well, I will certainly make sure that doesn't happen again." He paused to listen. "Today, right? And have there been any other days? Uh-huh." He nodded. "And has he been that way in other classes?"

Joey was done. Whether it was his teacher or the school social worker, he was done. He turned back to the game screen but didn't unpause it. He just couldn't stand to see Popop's face in that conversation anymore.

Popop hung up the phone. "Joy, getcha lil ass over here!" he yelled.

Joey sprinted over to the man's bedroom door.

"I hear you been cuttin school. Why the fuck wasn't you in school today?" He raised his voice even higher than Joey was already used to.

"Cause I—"

"You shut ya little faggot ass up!" he yelled, raising an arm.

"I didn't even—"

But his hand landed on the top of Joey's head so fast that the boy bit his tongue and his chin slammed into his chest.

"Fuck wasn't you in school?" Popop went on. "You do this shit every day? Fuck was you at?"

Joey said nothing. He was trying not to cry, but tears welled up fast, clumping into puddles at his eyes even though he refused to make a sound. He held in sobs and his body jerked in resistance. Then, that first sign of weakness, that slow tear rolled down his cheek.

"You better not start cryin neither," Popop said. Then he turned to Ganny a few feet away in his room. "Bitch, where was you at? You let this lil nigga stay off from school?"

"Earl, please," she said, not getting up from the bed. Her "please" was all the pleases combined. She meant "please" as in *please stop*. "Please" as in *nigga, please*, and "please" like the universal pleading, that desperation for anything, like sparing one's life.

"Please, my ass, you stankin bitch." Popop spat. "You ungrateful bitch. I'm tired of all yall in this fuckin house."

Joey didn't move but was looking down at a dark spot in the carpet. He could feel Popop moving again.

"Earl…" said Ganny, pleading. She rose from the bed to caress his hand and say it again. "Earl…" She turned her head slightly, gesturing him away from Joey and into their room.

"Don't touch me, you stank ass dirty ass bitch," he said. "Where the fuck was you at?" He raised his hand above his head again.

"Earl, please!" Ganny cried, covering her face with both hands.

Popop grabbed her wrists with his one big hand and smacked her down into the ground with the other. His face twitched with pride as she hit the floor.

"Earl, no!" Ganny screamed. Her voice broke. Joey moved closer to the couch and tried to look away, like always. Even though this happened often, and for different reasons—stealing, crack, sex with other men—Joey remembered this being the first time with a boot. He only saw Popop grab it from his periphery, the steel-toed black ones he'd walked around in all day at work. He brought the boot down on Ganny's body two or three times. She cried out. The sound crescendoed up into a heart-breaking pitch and then down into pure silence. Just her wide mouth pleading, with tears and snot running into it. She was miming her pain by then. Mika ran out to see what was happening, and Joey sent her back into the other room. The boy wept on the couch, hard and silent, while Ganny lay on the floor. The boy and the woman never looked at each other. Popop looked down on both of them, sour and out of breath. When he was finished, or had gotten too tired, he dropped the boot and walked back into his room. Ganny got up and went in after him.

"Now shut that door," Popop said. "You stankin ass bitch. Get over here and suck this dick."

It was then, listening to the slurping sound, that Joey truly learned the word "dick." He realized that a winkey was also something like a dick but smaller and nicer, even though it also meant "dick" sometimes. But "dick" was a bad word and a bad thing that only men had. Boys had winkeys, and he couldn't see himself growing into a man with a dick, like Popop. A dick meant fighting and hurt, hitting people in the face. Always. Drying his eyes, Joey went back to *Altered Beast* on Sega, transforming himself into a werewolf, a gargoyle, a bear, a werewolf, a gargoyle, a bear, over and over again, that demon overlord at the end of each stage sapping his powers away, laughing each time. But he kept starting over. Werewolf, gargoyle, and bear. And he was so tired by the time he finally beat the bear stage that he couldn't enjoy it. He fell asleep like that, right there on the couch.

When Joey awoke, Popop was already off to work. The boy got up starving and went straight into the kitchen for cereal. Mika popped out of bed as he passed the bedroom and followed him. She stood right behind him, hyper like every morning, bouncing on her toes like a boxer, waiting for him to pour her cereal.

"Wait, Mika," he said.

She poked her brother's arms and back with her skinny little fingers. "I'm hungry," she said.

Joey laughed. "Hungry, Mika. Wit a 'r,' like 'grrr.' "

"Grrrrr," Mika said.

Joey poured some King Vitaman into both their bowls and found the milk's expiration date was only two days before, September 17, 1996. Just in time. The little blue plastic bowls were stained orange, and they always felt greasy from microwaving those off-brand green cans of SpaghettiOs from Save-A-Lot. Joey packed them tight with little yellow crowns before Mika could complain that the bowls were dirty. He drowned them in milk and stood up in the kitchen eating. No one really used the old wood chairs in there except Mika because she couldn't reach the table otherwise. And then Joey saw them. Little black and brown bodies bubbling up to the surface, the whiteness of the milk making them impossible to ignore. Their antennae moved slowly as if slathered in molasses. The legs twitched. *Fuck*, Joey thought, wondering how many he'd already eaten. Mika found one and freaked out.

"Eill!" she yelled, dropping her spoon into the bowl, splashing the milk on the floor and table. She started crying.

Joey was just about to tell her to stop being a baby when Ganny must have heard and came into the kitchen. "Why ya sister cryin like that? What you do to that girl?" she asked.

Joey sighed.

Ganny examined the spilled milk on the table, the little roaches floating about in the bowls. "Stop playin," she said. "Act like yall ain't never ate no damn roaches before. And you gotta hurry up and get ready for school anyway, Joey."

One day, while cutting the grass outside Lustrik Corp., Joey came across a garter snake. At Birds, Birds, Birds they were $11.99 each, but here one was for free, unscathed by lawn mower blades, slithering right over the boy's foot. It was the biggest he'd ever seen, and the first brown one. He'd come across milk snakes and garters in the creek under the El down by KFC before, but never this close, this big, or this slow moving. He had to capture it. In his shortage of red-and-white-painted Pokeballs though, he simply picked the snake up and carried it down the street like a muscular strand of rope held up against his chest. He would name the creature Spike. He put Spike in an old pet cage, dusting away the remnants of fur, scales and cricket bodies he'd missed before, thinking he should have started with the snake and skipped all other animals prior. Joey gathered grass and dirt and filled Spike's water bowl, after letting the tap run a bit until it came out clear. Then he went right back down the street to cutting the grass, actively looking for snakes. Pushing through the field took twice as long but he found another one. Green this time. Big and juicy too, almost as large as the brown one. He named it Amy.

Amy was the first name that came to mind, the same name of this middle school girl Joey could not stop thinking about in such a way that it filled him with shame and consequently deepened his obsession. He wondered if it was appropriate for boys to think about girls this way, and if Popop ever thought this way too, and if so, what should he do to fix it? All of this was much more difficult to think about than just naming the snake Amy. So he named the snake Amy. The boy told everyone that these snakes were mutants because of how big they were. They were the Teenage Mutant Ninja Turtles of snakes rescued from a dreary life in some sewer, saved from hunting and gathering endlessly in the tall grass too. Joey knew that he could make the lives of these snakes better than even his own life and everybody he knew.

Standing at the top of his apartment building's three concrete steps to the front door Joey held Spike above his head how Rafiki did Simba; he could even hear "The Circle of Life" building up from the base of his skull, reminding him of where he'd come from and where he was about to go, foregone dreams of cartooning be damned, this snake and Joey would have a life together. A rapt audience of neighborhood kids—Kevin, Robby, Jeremy and Jeremy's older brother, Daniel—stared up in awe, all three of the African sisters from across the street—Erica, Maya, and the tiny one who always wore the Mickey Mouse pull-ups—stood with their mouths agape. Silence. Joey knew then, it was time to speak. "It is possible," he said, "that the chemicals from Popop job leaked into the grass and made these mutant snakes." The silence gave way to mumbling. "It's possible, is all I'm sayin." Then Joey looked around. "I'm matin these snakes," he said with Spike held high in his right hand. "And if yall want, yall can buy the babies from me." He stopped for a moment, considering a price. "Ten dollars each. They cost like twenty dollars at the pet shop. Yall can go check. I'm not even lyin."

Some of the kids, like Ray and Kevin, did actually fact-check Joey at the pet shop. It was summer, and it was only a block away on Frankford Ave. The girls, except Tia, went to go jump rope with Mika at the end of the street. Then, Tia came to hold Spike up to her face, flicking her tongue back and forth with his.

"Boy, you full of shit," she whispered to Joey.

But some of the boys were intrigued. Not necessarily Jeremy's brother Daniel, though, who was older and a self-proclaimed "wigger," so no one took him seriously. He had a lot of pimples like Tia, but his were red and violent looking, so Tia often called him pizza face, which somehow never eroded Daniel's extraordinary confidence.

"Joey, that's some bullshit. Fuck outta here," Daniel said.

"Whatever, Daniel," Joey replied. "You dumb anyway."

It would have scared Joey to say such a thing so assertively to anyone but Daniel. Though Daniel was older and stockier than all the other boys on Paul Street, he was still white, and when folks were being polite, they called him slow. He wasn't officially delayed as far as anyone knew, which made it seem okay to talk down to him about it; if Daniel was not officially delayed, but just mean or annoying, then he'd earned, as far as Joey was concerned, whatever offense could be given. That Joey probably couldn't beat him in a fight if it came down to it was beside the point. Daniel made Joey feel good, since he was living proof that Joey could be smarter than someone so much older than himself. That, and one summer, Daniel was attacked by a squirrel. It jumped straight off a tree and onto the center of his head and started gnawing and scratching like it was trying to dig through his scalp. For years, Joey joked that the only reason the squirrel left was because it couldn't find anything. Every time Joey called him dumb, Daniel just flagged the younger boy off and walked away. There were more comments on the snake before the door closed.

"So, you sayin them snakes is like the X-Men?" another boy asked.

In the apartment, Mika was not so fond of Spike or Amy, which Joey found entertaining. Whenever Mika fell asleep on the couch, she might jump up to an arm intertwined with a snake. Startled, she'd scream, "Joey, stop puttin them snakes on me!" An utterance that was sometimes linked to tears. Then Joey, unprompted, would try to show Mika that they weren't dangerous or scary as he guided her fingers along the outside of their enclosures or down their backs while Spike and Amy slithered around Joey's forearm, flicking their tongues like snakes do.

Tia loved them almost as much as Joey did but was quick and clear about the fact that they weren't her responsibility.

"Take care of ya animals," she'd always say, after kissing Spike or Amy on the face and letting them gently back into the cage. Ganny ignored them completely, shaking her head on occasion when she saw Joey sitting on the couch wearing snake necklaces. Popop said they would die. Hoped they would die. And Keisha thought they were just nasty. But this time, Joey gave his pets serious attention. He scraped the cage clean and scrubbed it from top to bottom. Then he got reptile mulch from the pet store. He collected rocks and twigs from the creek and made a pond for them, like the benevolent god of one big set piece. He stuffed the snakes on mealworms and crickets, spiders and pinkies, but they refused to eat the roaches. Then, when the snakes grew large enough, the Birds, Birds, Birds pet shop owner suggested feeding them mice, fresh or frozen. Joey wasn't quite ready to move so furrily up the food chain. He got goldfish, stocking them in the tiny pond he'd made inside the cage. The snakes could slurp them up at their leisure, safely. Live mice, by contrast, weren't passive prey. They fought back and bit out snake eyes, sometimes maiming or killing them, and Joey'd done such a good job with these snakes that he wasn't about to throw them away to *Pinky and the Brain*. And it paid off.

One morning Joey woke up to what looked like a few

slimy worms inside the snake cage. They kept wriggling out of Spike's body as he slithered around in circles, disseminating wet noodles one by one. They were covered in slime, like the residue slugs leave behind or that stuff between a Xenomorph's teeth when it opens wide to snarl and eat you. But there was something not right about it. Where were the eggs? Joey prided himself on knowing animals, both living and extinct, mammals and reptiles, lions and tigers and dragons and Poké-mon and GigaPets. He knew that snakes were supposed to lay eggs. That his snakes didn't was some kind of anomaly. Maybe they actually were mutant snakes, and his lie had contributed to something real. His story had embedded itself into reality and fundamentally altered it. Already, Joey was starting to believe his own myths, provide his own evidence where there might have been too little. He couldn't even count all the baby snakes in the tank, but he could definitely sell them. Two for twenty. With the money, Joey bought a larger tank and ate big turkey-and-cheese hoagies every day before dinner. Keisha was coming around every once in a while and asking for money, so he had to give her some. Popop suggested that he pay rent, and that was when Joey started acting like he wasn't making anything, saying instead that the snakes were dying or disappearing into the night.

Jeremy, just upstairs with his brother, was mad jealous. Their mom wouldn't let them have a snake at all, so he and Daniel came down to play with Spike and Amy sometimes. Daniel was clumsy with them and held them too tight, like a man choking someone. You could see the veins popping out of Daniel's wrist and hands, strangling the snakes, making Joey nervous, even though Daniel spoke as if he were calm, exerting no energy. *This level of force*, Joey thought, *must be normal for him.*

"What's this one's name again?" Daniel asked, clutching Spike in one hand.

"Spike," Joey said. "And the other one is Amy."

Then Daniel released them, finally, and held both arms out like a scarecrow, letting Spike slither from one end to the other as Joey put Amy back in the cage. As Spike coiled around Daniel's arm, he smiled a little.

"This snake ain't so tough," he said.

"What are you talkin about, Dan?" Jeremy asked, confused and squinting a little bit.

Until that moment, Joey hadn't considered the snake's toughness to be a core attribute, something he was supposed to be aware of and apparently foster. Daniel had this way of turning everything into a toughness competition, though. He wanted a pit bull, or some muscular dog, because they looked tough. He wanted tough-looking shirts and jewelry. He wanted all the boys to be tough. He was the older one, who, in the middle of sitting on the couch watching *Teletubbies* or *Care Bears*, would challenge Joey or Jeremy to a fight, grabbing Jeremy and putting him in a headlock. It annoyed Joey to no end, but at the same time he was glad that Jeremy was easier prey, being smaller and weaker, which meant less attention on himself. Still, Joey learned to play along when necessary. If he was forced into wrestling Daniel and lost, he'd insult the older boy to make himself feel better, like asking Daniel what grade he was in versus what grade he was supposed to be in, or pausing with great exaggeration during a video game or anime to read the text out loud and explain to Daniel what was going on. If Daniel didn't respond to this, Joey might invert the question.

"Hey Daniel, I'm sorry," he'd say. "Can you help me with these words?" Knowing damn well Daniel couldn't and how it ate away at him. The word "Leviathan" was a favorite. No matter how many times it came up.

But Jeremy couldn't resort to this strategy, or at least he never did. Daniel practiced wrestling moves on his little brother, saying them out loud as he laid hands on him.

"Oh!" he'd say. "The Stone Cold Stunner," or "Oh shit! The Chokeslam!" or "The Tombstone," with Jeremy's head between his legs or the boy's wiry neck in his hands. It happened so much that, half the time, Jeremy just lay still, flat faced and bored, asking Daniel to tell him when he was done.

Even though Joey knew these things about Daniel, he never expected these projections to land on the garter snakes. Spike, Daniel must have thought, needed to be a python or a cobra, something able to kill through strength or venom. The trepidation Joey felt at this was unbearable. *Why would anyone want to keep something like that?* he thought. His mind went to the fear he felt for Steve Irwin any time the man ran up on some snake or baby dragon in the outback and face-to-faced it barehanded and howling *crikey!* like he held some secret guarantee that everything would be fine. Joey just wanted pets he could hold. The fact that he could sell the babies was a pleasant bonus.

"This jawn did get big as shit," Daniel continued. "But it ain't tough like a real snake." Spike was longer than Daniel's arm, wrapped completely around it several times over.

"You can't even have no snake at all," Joey said, trying not to sound mad. "Your mommy won't let you."

Daniel turned to Joey real fast, aiming Spike's face at him. "I wouldn't get no bitch snake like this, though," he said, jabbing at Joey with Spike's head. "And at least I got a mom. Ya mom don't do nothin but wander around outside cracked out all the time."

Daniel opened the lid to put Spike back in his cage and the snake lunged at Daniel's pointer finger, clamping down on it up to the knuckle.

Daniel struggled to stay composed. "Joey," he said too slowly, "you better get this fuckin thing off me." His face was beet red, and he was breathing too fast.

Spike's jaw muscle was hard at work, squeezing and inching up Daniel's finger, trying to pull the whole worm of a thing into his gut. Joey didn't want to admit how pleased he was with this, how satisfying it was to see Daniel's fear and panic. The older boy's eyes were so wide, his whole body tense. Jeremy didn't hide his pleasure at all. He cackled nearly to death, rolling around on the dirty carpet holding his gut.

"Dan, you are such a fuckin punk," Jeremy said.

It took everything Joey had not to smile or laugh. He'd

been bitten by both Spike and Amy before. It hurt, sure, but not badly. It couldn't kill you. Daniel's officially revealed punk assness was the only explanation for his screaming and gesticulating with little purpose or thought like Jim Carrey in *The Mask*. It was almost like this was the first time Daniel had ever really felt pain. *Daniel sweet as shit*, Joey thought, but he tried to keep his composure. "Dan, just calm down and he'll let go," Joey said.

But Daniel flailed around and slapped the snake all over the place. Spike's tail hit Joey in the face like a whip. Jeremy dodged it. Daniel's panic kept increasing.

"What the fuck!" Joey said. "Just calm down and I can get him off. Calm the fuck down, dummy!"

Daniel ran out the front door. Joey and Jeremy gave chase. Outside it was still warm; the weather felt like just a few minutes before someone might crack open the fire hydrant. Mika and them were playing hopscotch in the street and a group of boys were playing free ball with a smashed huggie juice bottle right next to them. Tia had been watching Mika from the window, but turned her eye to the snake ruckus when Daniel burst outside, Joey yelling after him.

"Daniel, calm down!" Joey said. But that only seemed to agitate him more. Jeremy was standing back as Daniel entered the middle of the street, still whipping around and struggling with the snake. Kids froze to stare at him. Every time Joey tried to approach and get Spike off he had to dodge the tail. He could never get close enough. Both he and Daniel were frustrated and sweating. Joey thought about just going for Daniel's neck and trying to choke him out, taking a few lashes from the snake tail as necessary. He was standing just out of Daniel's reach, ebbing back and forth, waiting for a chance to jump in like he was playing double dutch. But then Daniel started beating the snake's body against the curb. Flecks of blood and scales, still green and sparkling, peppered Joey's face. Some got in his mouth because he was yelling for Daniel to stop.

"Just stop! Please," he said. "Stop!"

Joey lunged at Daniel. But just then the snake slipped off Daniel's finger. He was still flailing with all his might, though, and as Spike's whole body loosened up, Daniel sent the snake sliding right into the sewage drain. How the boy wished this happened in slow motion. Joey dove in after Spike as deep as he could, his face pressed up against the curb, clawing and grasping at nearly nothing, as the tip of the snake's tail slipped down into what Joey just knew was a crocodile-infested sewer. Spike was gone. Joey stayed there trying for ten or fifteen minutes just reaching, hoping that Spike would reach back up for him, too. By the time Joey stood up, Daniel was standing right behind him rubbing the injured finger. There was a little droplet of blood.

"You see," Daniel said, "what your fuckin snake did to me?"

According to local authorities, there was little Joey, the boy, could do which was not gay and therefore worthy of reprimand. Brushing his teeth was too gay because of that in-and-out motion; listening to R&B, which Joey loved, with Maxwell or Chilli singing in his ear, was too gay because why would you let some R&B nigga sing in your ear all smooth like that? And if it were Chilli, why would you allow some girl to control your feelings like that? Washing and smelling nice was too gay because that was what girls did; eating popcorn was too gay because they were just busted nuts. Walking or running for exercise was gay because men lifted weights. Wearing flip-flops like the Ninja Turtles was gay because those were thong flip-flops. Breathing was too gay because that meant you were alive.

And so on.

Perhaps this stricture seemed so gross, coming from people who also said they loved Joey, because even he didn't understand where to find it in his own body. It indicated, for him, an impossibility between them. Their obsession with who he was, the fact of it, was just too deeply ingrained despite its lack of truth content, and yet this was the only part of him worth seeing. The distance between himself and his family then was impossible. And what did he desire? Besides wanting to be left alone on occasion, to be touched more gently by others, and to play? The unknown unknowns were still around except that whatever he did want could only ever be a surprise. How to extricate himself?

Perhaps the least surprising desire, then, was that Joey wanted to die. He hardly told anyone at home or at school, but that was only because it was already so obvious. It might be better. He figured well, Raziel was dead and having a much better time than Joey in *Soul Reaver*. With Joey in *Soul Reaver*. Perhaps it was an opportunity. He let it slip to a social worker once, which earned him a beating, and later he told a therapist who found it kind of funny. *So fuck it*, he thought, *I'll laugh, too.*

"But you're such a big, strong boy, and so smart for your age," the lady said. "Why in the world would you want to do something like that?"

And Joey laughed and laughed and went back to being Raziel.

He pulled his shirt up over his mouth like his bottom jaw was missing, making it hard to tell him and the dead and dreary vampire servant apart. And how could the old, dead vampire complain anyway at a second chance? Lined up to take revenge or snatch souls, but, most importantly, be left alone if he wanted. Because what's fate without a little privacy? He'd roam the empty halls of the spectral realm for life if it meant this kind of peace. Up and down the halls they'd walk. Up and down the halls.

But at his most defeated, he would mention it to Popop, threatening almost, begging someone to help him do it after watching Ganny beaten, or being ordered to bed still hungry or whatever other mundane sissy gripe he had.

"Do it then, you little faggot," Popop said. "Fuckin do it, sissy. All fuckin talk. Fuck outta here."

And maybe he was all talk, since it would take so long, much after the ending of this particular fable, to even try. Seeing Kain's whole empire in shambles wasn't enough. Centuries of failed attempts at correction. And here Joey was being taught that writing was just another form of talk. And so he took Raziel and leapt from the tallest crag rock he could find.

"Your wings, though ruined," God said, "are not without purpose. Take hold of them as you leap, and they will carry you across this chasm."

And so Joey and Raziel died together. And got back up with a slight reduction of faith.

Even though he would outgrow that monkey boy Goku, Joey couldn't help but love the little pervert's endless pool of grit. Toonami had him wide open to all things *Dragon Ball Z*, and not an episode went by where Goku, hair sharp and bright and glistening, had not gotten his ass beaten to near oblivion. But he fought through it, and kept fighting. He was abandoned, had no family, no history, no origin that could be readily narrated to anyone he knew. There was no one yelling at the top of their lungs about how much they loved him, either. And so he went through it. But there was always something in his back pocket, something more, unseen and indescribable, just when you thought he'd reached his limit. Just when he'd been tested so thoroughly that no human or even Saiyan should have survived, he'd turn the whole thing around. Goku literally died all the time trying to save his new friends, his found family, his new planet, and returned all the stronger for it. This, and what quickly began to feel like empty and far-too-heroic dialogue between fights that spanned several episodes made the plot laughable, but gave Joey room to consider much better ones.

Goku was among the first people, or things, that Joey wished to be rather than deal with his own inadequate body. He had the weakest bird chest on the block, smaller than those parakeets—lovebirds, Popop called them—that the old man kept in the living room next to the fish tank. Goku had pecs. Joey's uncles had pecs. Popop had one of those hairy animal chests that women found sexy. On a good day, Joey's chest might be compared to a cartoon skeleton. All skin and bones and pussy boy, people said. But when he finally started puberty, stretching out like Gumby, or some Play-Doh snake rolled too long in a toddler's palms, the only part that widened was his chest. Not pecs, though. He swore he was growing titties like a girl. These tight little popped-out nubs that hurt whenever he tried to touch them. Standing in front of the mirror, he'd finger the little rocks on his chest, recoiling at the pain of whatever dense ball of iron might be stuck in there.

Tia found it entertaining. She'd burst into the bathroom, smiling ear to ear, a wide glare shining from her glasses and say, "See, told you you was a girl."

"Whatever," Joey'd reply. "My titties gonna be bigger than yours then."

"You so stupid," Tia went on. "Good for you."

People called Tia a tomboy because she had no titties and wore braids like A.I., even though she was corny at basketball. She rode trick bikes all the time, too, and only hung out with boys. Whenever another girl her age or even older called Tia a tomboy, she made jokes about fucking their boyfriends, which Joey later learned were not jokes at all but plain statements of fact. The boy was in awe at how Tia dismantled the personhood of a bully without breaking a sweat or having to get beat up. They tended to cry and run away while Tia kept a straight face. She was so small, too, always under ninety pounds, which suggested to Joey that an enemy could have killed her if they'd ever had the heart to try. Joey couldn't tell if it was because Popop threatened to shoot anyone who touched his daughter, or if Tia had some kind of psychic power over them. When this younger girl, one of Mika's friends, got caught making fun of Tia's pimples, Tia said, "Well, ya dad is too busy eatin this pussy to notice." And it wasn't even scandalous. The girl cried and tried to snitch, but everybody was like *Oh, that's just Tia*. And life went on. In this way, Tia was the second person that Joey wanted to be.

With regard to the titties, Popop just told Joey to shut up and stop touching himself. He was paranoid, prodding the little rock nubs, eventually settling on the fact that he had a rare instance of male breast cancer. He knew, beyond the shadow of a doubt, that he would die any day from the throbbing nodules lodged in his otherwise scrawny chest. Such fear led him to ask his mother about it the next time she was around.

"Boy, stop bein so ridiculous," she said.

"I'm not," Joey replied. "Look at this!" And Joey raised his shirt, which was white with orange stains from SpaghettiOs, up over one nipple. "Look!" he pointed to the right-nipple anomaly.

Keisha fell over laughing.

"It's not funny!" he said. Then he couldn't help but smile at the way his mother was enjoying herself. It was such a rare scene, and the boy would go on to try and re-create it whenever he caught her sober.

Eventually, the rock nubs would spread out and flatten. But, for the time being, whenever Mika and Joey and Tia sat in front of the TV watching *Dragon Ball*, the two girls would chuckle at naked baby Goku.

"Like Joey's chest," Mika would say.

The boy sat there, side-eyeing them. "And when he turn into the big monkey, that's you," he said to his sister, lifting up the back of her shirt to check for a tail. But even baby Goku, in the old Technicolor cartoon, had a stronger chest than Joey. It was a compliment, really, drawing the comparison. He should have been proud.

Joey wondered how the kids at school would react if they knew he stood on his couch, hands clasped tight behind him, powering up Kamehameha energy blasts, or strained himself to death trying to turn Super Saiyan. He wanted so badly to do something through sheer force of will and anger—there was so much of it, just overflowing—but he had neither the know-how nor the heart to put it to good use. Nothing looked more invigorating than to smash some obvious bad guy to pieces, to cut their arms and legs off and play with them, to ask Popop, after an epic defeat, if he'd had enough of Joey's hands with one foot on the man's chest. Just thinking of it lifted the boy's spirits up some days, just above the level of wanting to end his own life. He got really good at shooting things from his hands like they were energy blasts. He stood on the living room couch and waited for Mika to walk in and bang! Tennis ball Kamehameha to the head. Bang! Knocked her down with a couch pillow.

Standing on the couch was supposed to be like flying, but he never quite worked the logistics out. He spent hours explaining to Mika how she should fall or fight back when hit with a particular type of energy blast, Big Bang Attack, Galick Gun, Spirit Bomb, Death Beam; they each required a different kind of coordination and response, like you couldn't avoid a Spirit Bomb (big couch pillow) by just rolling two feet to the side. You had to block it with another energy blast, or it would destroy the whole planet and make the brown carpet turn to lava and everybody would die. But say, Special Beam Cannon, you could just dodge by sidestepping. Mika mostly smiled and giggled, and said Joey was cheating if he ran home from school first and threw the pillows at her as she walked in, before she had a chance to put her book bag down. *She's not taking it seriously enough*, Joey thought. She thought they were playing a game, like kids. Joey started trying to run like anime characters did, too, his arms dragging behind him as if he were moving so fast that some of his body would get left behind. And maybe it did.

At night, Joey kept having these vivid dreams where he was

flying, directionless mostly, but always with some pure and diffuse goal in mind. It was all revolution and fire and good and evil, dragons and giants, and mean and nice and sometimes just open, dark sky like Sega Saturn *Nights*. In these dreams Joey had neither the complications of childhood nor the responsibility for other people's adulthood. He'd wake up on the floor in the morning, crying like always. Not because he was hurt, but just because he realized that he could not, would not, ever fly. In those moments he knew that everything he thought or cared about was, and would always be, objectively meaningless in the near and distant futures. Mornings were hard to breathe. He could find no humans in life to prove breathing and being worthwhile, and he began to admire only the dead, wishing to be one of them more every day. And there were just too many examples about how death wasn't forever. *Return stronger, better*, he thought. Forget looking under skirts or catching glimpses of young Chi-Chi's titties, what Joey wanted was Goku's life over death, long monkey tail or not. Struggling, he sometimes allowed hope to pour in from the imaginary, from anime and video games which did not replicate real life but speculated so astronomically about what could be that they created the only space within which he could not predict a lightless future.

Even though Joey left *Dragon Ball Z* at home because he knew better, the most important lessons in grade school were also about violence. Stearne Elementary was less than a block away from the apartment on Paul Street, at the intersection with Unity. It was next to a church where Joey sometimes sat through Bible study begrudgingly, frustrated with the lack of answers or honesty, thinking about how it was the same as school. While standing on the schoolyard asphalt, wishing it was like the endless fields of grass he'd seen on TV, he could stare over at the brown bricked apartment where he and his family lived. A few trees lined the other side of the street in front of the Post Office. Their changing leaves would float into the yard through a nine-foot fence and decorate the concrete. Joey particularly liked the yellow-orange leaves of fall, ones with little holes in them. He would gather them up looking for signs of life. Which holes were made by caterpillars, and which by fungus or decay? And did it matter? Did someone burn holes in them with a match, for no real reason? As contained as the schoolyard felt when the gates were locked, there was a child-sized hole on the far end of it that, among other things, the teachers never seemed to notice.

The hole was important, and sometimes Joey showed up late and walked through it into school, instead of through the gate with the other kids. There were big gray metal doors that were hard to open, like they were made for minotaurs or something, leading to his third-grade classroom. The school looked like it should have metal detectors, but didn't yet. Outside, all the kids lined up in size order, waiting to enter while taking off their jackets. As tall as a middle schooler already, Joey brought up the rear. In the classroom he put his coat on the floor beneath the others because there were never any more hooks. He was annoyed, though, because it had a little hole in the arm that he kept trying to tape shut; it spilled fluff haphazardly. He'd learned how important it was to find the most inconspicuous seat in the room anyway; even though he imagined that sitting up front was more conducive to learning, it was too risky. The tall lanky kid in the front of class with the bowl cut, the huge gap between his rotted front teeth, and clothes that smelled of urine was too easy a target; even Joey hated him. God forbid the roaches crawled out of his jacket or book bag again. Their little brown bodies scurrying across the white classroom floor were hard to miss. But Joey thought that if he could go without incident for a week or two straight, maybe some kids would forget.

He found a seat on the far left column of desks, in the middle row. It was perfect. He could see the chalkboard clearly and it was right next to the coat rack, so he might be able to squash any roaches crawling out this time before anyone noticed. The hallway door was close too, and he always needed to go to the bathroom, but didn't want to draw attention to himself by raising his hand and asking. Joey could hear his heart thrumming into his ears just considering it, how the other students would notice something wrong with him as soon as he got up: pants too tight, stains on his shirt, standing like a girl, sitting like a girl, letting out too much slack on his wrists like a gay boy. It was always something. On the day in question, his teacher made reference to one of the DARE posters, which had been smeared on all four walls of every classroom the boy could remember. She rattled off all of the evil things she knew about drugs and, by association, the people who used them.

"'Drug Abuse Resistance Education,'" the teacher said,

pointing to the cartoon lion mascot wearing the black-and-red shirt, "is what 'DARE' stands for. An officer will come to class and talk to us tomorrow, but can anybody tell me how we stay away from drugs today?"

Joey was underwhelmed and started to nod off a little. The teacher noticed it a few times and told him to pay attention. He was so tired that he kept dozing, though, his head bobbing up and down, in and out of reality, until a tight and practiced smack landed on the back of his neck. Joey cringed and his muscles stiffened. It burned more inside his gut than outside on his skin.

He knew exactly what to do, how he should react. But he didn't have the heart. He heard it often. *You ain't got no heart*, from everybody, so it had to be a little true. He'd calculated the best possible outcome in this smacking scenario hundreds of times and, on each occasion, failed to act. Had he gotten up wordlessly and punched the first kid in the mouth who sat behind him, girl or boy, his entire grade school existence would have changed. This would no longer be his *Groundhog Day*. And the frustration lay in the fact that Joey didn't completely know why he couldn't do it, heart or no heart. Maybe it was because Popop liked physical violence so much and Joey hated him. Maybe Joey just thought he was too good for it, or shouldn't have to consider it at all.

The usual chatter froze in the slap's echo. It was like no matter how many times it happened, it was always new. The sound stood out more than Joey ever could have on his own. To his ears, it was still just as loud as when it happened. His heart sank like always, dropped into the pit of his stomach. The teacher stopped writing on the blackboard and speaking for just a second to look around, her lips pursed. Then came the muffled giggles and chuckles of what felt like the entire school behind him, a pack of starving hyenas. Some, it seemed, were struggling to hold in their joy. Other mouths exploded, their little child hands too weak to contain the excitement. And Joey had to admit that if it were someone else in his position, and he wished this, that he would have laughed if only to hide his relief, never looking in the other kid's face. Every hurt person who wasn't him was its own small victory. Sometimes the only victory. He'd known that feeling when he watched another kid get beaten up, slapped, or punched, when his little sister got blamed for things instead of him, even though Popop didn't hit her—and sometimes even when Ganny was beaten. It was unavoidable. Human survival dictated that a lot of people got hurt for other people to feel good and alive. Knowing this, he stared straight ahead without blinking, focusing on his breathing, trying to relax. Each time it happened, he lasted a little longer before the tears. Joey hated those kids for being who they were but, had he any heart, he would have traded places with them in a second.

"Cut the tomfoolery!" the teacher yelled. It was her favorite word. "Tomfoolery." She addressed the whole class, rather than single out the slapper or the slapped. Joey's teacher must have imagined this as the best thing to do, must have seen it in a handbook or been told about it at a meeting. Then she turned back to the blackboard and continued writing as if nothing happened. Joey was hyperaware of how different everyone's worlds must be. For his teacher, it was just another day at her job: kids slapping, not working, saying drugs are bad, and then maybe going home to her own family, a husband, some happy-smiley kids, or maybe her second job. The thought of it funneled Joey into a murderous rage. He had to do something different before he was officially a grown-up, too, because how would that work?

A few minutes passed. The excitement died down, and Joey snuck a shirtsleeve across his face once or twice, wiping his eyes in secret. Someone must have noticed, though, because right after he did that, three coordinated, consecutive hands came across the back of his neck and head, twice as hard as before. Startled, he poked himself in the eye with his own finger before his forehead slammed against the desk from the final slap.

"Open neck, no respec, you fuckin faggot!" one of the kids behind him yelled out.

"Didn't I say cut it out?!" The teacher turned around again, this time raising her voice a little higher. Joey's head throbbed as he struggled not to cry. But his high-water pants were filling up. Urine warmed his thighs, and the release at first was soothing. And the tears came, despite himself. He lost control of his bowels, too. Shit squeezed its way into the plastic seat with him. Everything was warm. He should have just gotten up and used the bathroom beforehand. He should have sat somewhere else, maybe all the way in the back where it was safe, with no one behind him. He should have stopped going to school altogether, a long time ago. And then the other kids noticed the mess. They smelled things. This cute Puerto Rican girl Joey had a crush on was the first to take a stand.

"Eeiill, he pooped on his self!" she yelled, as if rallying troops on a battlefield.

The rest of the class followed her lead, and Joey must have been called every word relating to shit, piss, nasty, dirty, smelly, sissy, and gay a few times over, all words he already knew well. Always gay for some reason. The teacher waited it out as usual. She looked into the crowd of misbehaving children as if a plan of action might drop into her lap from the atmosphere. The chanting continued until Joey decided to leave. He felt dumb being there in the first place. Speed-walking out of the classroom was the best way to do it; running—showing any more thoroughly that he cared, or was hurt—would make things worse; of course they had him, but maybe how much they knew they had him could be reduced if he got away cool enough. He did run, though, as soon as he hit the schoolyard, right through the gate hole, cutting his winter jacket open wider by sliding through too fast. As he sped up, the wet pants got cold and hard on his way to the apartment.

He opened the door with a sigh of relief before smelling the smoke. Popop was definitely home. Joey didn't expect this in the middle of a weekday. Nine to five. Those were the hours he was supposed to be at work. Nine to five. Joey coughed and wheezed, and his underarms sweated, smelling like raw onions. Popop had been passed out in bed when Joey stormed in. The way he jumped up, and his expression, told Joey that the man could not believe someone swung through the door like that in the middle of the day. The man was supposed to be taking a break, it seemed, and Joey had brought his time with no kids or Ganny or work or anyone crashing down. Popop rose to his feet with such violence that Joey thought he'd be killed before any cursing or conversation that might half explain himself. Standing inches away from the boy's face he said real slow, "What the fuck you think you doin home from school, little nigga?"

"Popop, I couldn't stay there, they—"

And he slapped Joey upside the head. "I ain't tryna hear all that little faggot shit," Popop said. "Why you ain't in school?"

Popop's beard and tightly trimmed box haircut were just starting to add a touch of gray then, and his teeth looked like mangled candy corn with refrigerator mold on them. His breath normally smelled of alcohol, but the smoke wrapped around his whole person and stomach, and chest hair poked through the little holes of his fishnet belly shirt.

Trying to avoid a second blow, Joey backed away from him a little before speaking again. "I was in school, but they—"

Popop lunged quicker than Joey expected of an old man and smacked him on the top of his head again. Then, he sniffed the air, his nose twitching like a dog. He frowned. He grimaced. "Just shut the fuck up and get your little nasty ass in the shower," Popop said. "Out here smellin like shit. Always whining about something, ungrateful little bitch. Don't you know the shit I deal wit takin care of you? You think ya skank ass Ganny gone do it if I wasn't here? What about that bitch Keisha? Where ya mom at? I don't see her in here takin care of yall. So fuckin ungrateful, spoiled ass kids. Watch, one day I'm not gone be around, and you gone regret this shit…"

Popop kept mumbling insults while Joey undressed in the bathroom, trying not to smear anything. When his voice faded, Joey still knew what he was saying, grinning at the measly ass limits of his vocabulary. *I'm a lot smarter than him*, Joey thought. *At least I have that.* And this also made him ashamed. Water boiled on the stove, and Popop slid the warm water pot into the bathroom without a word. In it, Joey dumped dishwashing liquid and a bag of plastic army men. There was a really muscular, well-jointed Spider-Man figure, too. He locked the door before grabbing a giant rubber snake he'd gotten from the trick shop. The snake, a giant, messed-up evolutionary experiment from Cobra HQ—"evolutionary" being another one of Joey's favorite words—was attacking the legion of plastic army men whose feet were unfortunately molded into flat platforms; this was due to a curse from ancient times, even though they blamed Cobra HQ for that too. They'd hidden in the swamp, the soapy bucket, and called giant Spider-Man for help, who then went to work on the anaconda cobra creature. But Spider-Man was too weak, and in his dying moments, all seventy-three "for children over seven years of age" army men shot their mortars and rifles and pistols and grenades at the snake, finally overpowering it. They danced and cheered in their victory, and sang "Enter Sandman" in unison holed up around a scented candle, upon which they would roast the snake's body and feast for years to come. But it was too late for giant Spider-Man. Overcome by his injuries, he collapsed into the swamp. The army men ate him, too.

Popop came to the door but Joey had already locked it. "Fuck you doin in there, Josephine. Open the door. I ain't mean to yell at you like that."

Joey froze. Staring at the toilet, he let his eyes relax, lose focus. He fantasized about Popop dying—of killing the old man with his own gun. He drank too much and slept enough, so it wouldn't be hard. Writing his name and wishing wasn't working. The gun was in the ceiling tile right above the bed, too, fourth one from his door diagonally. *It would not be that hard*, Joey thought. *It should not be this hard.*

INTERLUDE

Things aren't exactly looking up for our heroes, folks: the army men, the rats, the cats, the snake, the dog, the boy. What will they do? What will the boy do with them? Will he dispatch his foes with Popop's ceiling-tile gun? Will he develop gumption and introspection to such an extent that he might become an entrepreneur of the self, extricating his own body from the tyrannical unfairness of antisocial life? Will he articulate a nuanced critique of structural injustices centering on the violence of cis-white heteropatriarchy and publish said study through a professional press, therefore saving not only himself but the world from such dangers? Will he simply grow up, come of age, and forget all about it in order to pen a more insightful story about the many nuances of Black joy despite his own subjective experience, overcoming individuality in the service of lifting every voice to singing? Or will he simply die, having succeeded in a dying world where success almost always means someone else's dying? Find out next time, on *Dragon Ball Z*.

A my just wasn't the same after Spike died, and neither was Joey. She fell ill, or Joey became too depressed to care for her, and she grew stiff and died alone. Popop noticed the smell and then Joey's excessive sadness, which, all things considered, wasn't much more excessive than before except for the fact that now Joey expended less energy hiding it. Popop had never liked the snakes, but Joey's excessive sadness made him uncomfortable, maybe because it represented a failure within himself to keep the house up either in order or appearance. This was how Joey ended up with the dog Blacky.

Blacky was technically an outside dog, a black Labrador retriever who, since there was no outside, was relegated to the basement like some kind of wild yet cuddly devil. Blacky was somewhat of a gift, a combination of Popop's guilt at being unable to satisfy Joey's emotional needs nor make him strong enough to ignore them, and a neighbor's dog who seemed to always be having puppies, most of whom ended up as strays and were later killed when they bit someone's kid on the face. But

Blacky wasn't like that, at first. With much enthusiasm, the little puppy was mostly interested in licking Joey's face, wrestling on the floor, eating, and shitting. There was something soothing in Blacky's comportment, "comportment" being another one of Joey's favorite words, circa *Buldar's Gate* or *Gauntlet* or one of those overhead party RPG games where such words came up inevitably in a tavern just before you decide whether or not to beat some drunk NPC's ass as he disrespects the women in your party, mistaking them for a prostitute or you for a vagabond. Though maybe "soothing" isn't the right word to describe an animal who grew more wild and more puppylike as he gained in size. It felt good to hold and squeeze something so large and permanent, nearly indestructible, and warm.

It didn't take long, though, before Joey couldn't even walk Blacky on his own. No matter how much he begged, it was a joke that someone might lend a hand. *You wanted that stupid fuckin dog*, they said. *It ain't my dog, take care of ya responsibilities for once.* And so Blacky spent even more time in the basement, his shit and piss accumulating no matter how much Joey tried to clean it up. There were piles everywhere like when your Digimon pooped in *Digimon World*, but less cute, with textures from soft-serve ice cream to bricks of ice. Everyone else avoided the basement, for the smell, for the big dog down there who was now a bad dog because of how excited he was, how desperate for attention. Joey wished he could stay home from school and cater to Blacky; he tried to do push-ups and get strong enough to take him out, but it never worked. The more time Blacky spent alone in the basement, the further he grew away from being a pet and more into a wild animal. He'd be smothered in his own excrement, all over his face and paws, barking all day and night, and he'd cry when Joey came down to feed and pet him and cry when Joey left for school or went to bed. The dog rubbed his nose up against the door while the children slept on the other side, never quite able to become part of the family or sleep in the apartment. But Blacky was sturdy. He'd survive. He would definitely make it.

Even though it hurt that Joey had to give Blacky away, he knew it was for the best. *At least he didn't die*, the boy kept thinking. That Blacky might live a normal life out on a cartoon pasture meant the amelioration of Joey's guilt. *At least he didn't die.* And as Joey got bigger, he kept wondering if he was yet strong enough to walk Blacky himself and whether he should try and get him back. Was there a court he could appeal to? How long do those dogs live anyway? And even if Blacky could return, would he still feel the same?

Joey failed with plenty of pets after that: fire belly newts, two lizards, an iguana, those guinea pigs, red-eared sliders, found toads, funny-looking frogs, mice, rats and gerbils, milk snakes, an angry praying mantis, hermit crabs, and a brown ferret. He always knew he'd find more. There were always more animals to touch and to love and to squeeze, and to die before their time. How could he learn to love something? It seemed that everywhere he looked, love was not allowed, save for the people who looked like him on television but were obviously always lying about how happy they were and who had to die for them to be happy. He thought wolf spiders had more answers than those people.

Joey grabbed two wolf spiders from the patio, the largest ones he could find, and put them in an arena with a house centipede, a few roaches, and a white mouse with red eyes. The mouse was only a dollar, and the brown mice in the house were difficult to catch and quick to bite, unlike the carefree feeder white mouse, who mostly shat in Joey's hand or on his neck as it nuzzled up against him. The arena results were unexpected. The mouse didn't do much of anything except back away, a coward. Everyone ignored the roaches. They always ignored the roaches. One wolf spider left and the other attacked the house centipede, grappling and piercing into it as the centipede wrapped its whole body around the spider in a begging embrace. It bucked and whipped against the spider's furry legs until finally, twisting and turning the thing around, they both expended themselves completely. Tired and gnawed on, they gave up slowly, twitching still, their muscles clenched on each other until all movement ceased.

Then, the mouse ambled over and nibbled both their heads off. The whole scene was what Joey might have described as evolutionary, the word Joey still loved but had come to understand as something inherently evil depending on who you asked. But he kept staging and watching these arena fights and called himself learning. His age being in the double digits now and having composed himself to no longer piss the bed, he figured that were Blacky around in this very moment, he'd be able to do right by him. And that was when he saw it, browsing the pet store for the last time, the alligator. A dream come true, a whole dragon in the flesh, something ancient and invincible for real, and much cooler than anything one could normally call a pet. He would definitely capture and train it himself, as soon as he was ready.

A hundred dollars ain't even that much for a whole alligator, Joey thought, walking up Frankford Avenue clutching rusted bills in one hand, feeling the other crumpled-up ducats secure in his left sock.

"Always keep your money in two separate places," Popop liked to say.

And Joey remembered. He'd forgotten, though, that Philadelphia is a city of great seasons, that he himself had caught cold, then pneumonia, and nearly died at some children's hospital no thanks to his own body's shallow attempts at thermo regulation. He was forgetting weakness in favor of developing strength. The alligator was a part of that. And it was warm out now, the perfect temperature for an alligator. It was getting warmer all the time. *And nothing lasts forever anyway*, Joey thought. Best to get an alligator now before it was too late and put everything else off until later, if later ever came.

The balding Chinese man at Birds, Birds, Birds was too excited about selling an alligator to Joey to inform him about care. He'd seen enough Animal Planet to know what alligators did anyway. Most of Joey and the man's chats had centered on Joey's questions, which always had to do with how big the various animals got and whether he could cuddle them or not. And even if the man would have said anything in caution, it's likely that Joey would have simply ignored him, knowing far better than to trust an adult. Nothing but lies and trickery, self-exceptions, excuses for why he should show them deference but they never needed to show him respect, and so on. Either way, Joey had saved up ninety-nine dollars and ninety-nine cents from cutting grass and shoveling snow with a patience he would run out of long before his own adulthood. This was long after he'd spent the money from hustling baby garter snakes on cheesesteaks and blue sodas, double cheeseburgers, and stockpiles of freeze-dried, shrimp-flavored noodles in Styrofoam cups. He spent his twenty-dollar allowance mostly on food, too. Before that, sure, he'd dabbled in geckos and newts for a while, considered a savannah monitor, a black-and-white tegu twice, and even had an iguana named Lizzie in between. But an alligator, to have and to hold, would be the kind of real and otherworldly satisfaction that Joey had longed for through all the other dead animal bodies.

Its name would be Rex. This sounded more prehistoric, like the way Rex looked. Eyes like amber with a slit down the center, Rex's teeth and jaws and skin and claws rugged like those car tires sitting in that lot across the street. It was clear to Joey that Rex was not the type to desiccate easily, "desiccate" being yet another one of Joey's favorite words ever since *Icewind Dale*, when your party discovers the remains of a massive sea dragon "desiccated" atop a great, snowy mountain. Joey pondered what this said about geological time and naively gathered the courage once to ask this question during a block of grade school science instruction.

Nevertheless, Joey dug a hole in the forbidden backyard right above where he'd buried Quaily. Poor Quaily. There were no bones, no trace of the old dead bird. Its skeleton, so brittle, had become one again with that planet beneath the tread of Joey's FILAs, those sneakers that Tia called Faggots in LA. Joey wanted to honor Quaily's memory, but it was like Quaily had never existed. He couldn't even remember the strange noises it made, only that they were strange. And alligators need ponds, maybe even a moat, actually, something like Guts and Griffith had built to protect the Band of the Hawk. *Berserk* needed only suggest dealing with the devil for paradise to muddy up the boy's moral superiority. And Griffith knew, that skinny little flamboyant boy who made it, who fucked and made friends, who conquered and protected, who made himself unforgivable in the end: we must abolish the dead to make space for the living. It was from this kind of forward thinking that the boy's pride would emerge. Joey measured and dug the pond over Quaily's grave to be three feet deep by however wide his imagination might carry it. The dig alone took more than a whole day, but Joey woke up early and rushed through it.

There were scarcely any kids outside, and the sun waned as Joey walked home with a whole alligator in tow. Rex's scaly body rested the length of his forearm, with a rubber band tied twice around his snout like a muzzle. Joey felt bad about this and reassured Rex that they would be home soon and he'd remove it. Rex was about the size that Lizzie the iguana was when she died, and just as inactive, but with a meatier tail. Joey put Rex down in the dry pond and loosened the band from his mouth. The creature just stared at him, blinking slowly. Then Joey turned on the garden hose and filled the pond with water. Unlike Blacky, who tore everything up and barked and disturbed the neighbors, Rex didn't budge, and the boy could sense neither joy nor trepidation from his new friend. So he sprayed Rex with the hose a little, trying to get a rise out of him. The water splashed off Rex's snout and eyes, but he remained calm. The most he would give Joey was turning around to be sprayed in the back instead. Then, once the pond was adequately transformed into mud, Rex just walked away from it.

Joey sprang into action, grabbing Rex by his soft belly, placing him back in the pond where he'd be safe. The myriad encounters where baby gators were eaten by birds or snakes on Animal Planet flashed before his eyes and made his heart pump faster; sweat dripped down his face.

"Stay," Joey said. And Rex did. In that moment, Joey had even begun losing faith in Steve Irwin, who seemed always to struggle with alligators, all mounting and tackling and yelling.

Rex was calm. Gazing down at his creation, Joey saw that it was good. He thought to himself, *Rex will have a ball swimming around in there*, eating snakes and lizards and whatever fish the boy might toss in for him.

But it was getting dark fast, and something told Joey that Rex should not be outside alone at night. He worried that those demons from *Where the Wild Things Are*, or even the Teletubbies themselves, might show up and squash or eat his alligator. Inside, Rex lived in the old lizard cage, filled mostly with water and some of the prettier rocks Joey had found while scavenging for turtles in the creek. Rex spent a lot of time in the cage because the pond didn't work out quite like Joey had planned; it was one big pile of mud that would dissolve and need to be refilled constantly. Sometimes, when Rex was out there, Joey had to dig into the mud blind to find him, wading through the thickness fingers first, feeling the squish of uncertainty slide up through the ridges of his palm. On hotter days Joey might find Rex lying dry in the pond's center with his mouth wide open. Popop yelled at Joey for wasting so much water, too, but it was a worthwhile complication to keep Rex happy. If it was too hot, Joey left the water hose running from the alley to the backyard all day until Popop got home from work.

Rex would eat almost anything. His favorite food, though, was the chubby goldfishes from the pet shop. But they were pricey. Not the little flat-booty, always-orange goldfish one could buy, say, two for a dollar. Rex needed the big, juicy ones with bug eyes that came in different colors; they cost anywhere from one dollar to three dollars each; and it was lost on no one that Joey was spending the same amount of money on goldfish that he could have spent on dollar hoagies and cheesesteaks, combined with the nerve to say that he was hungry, like it was someone else's responsibility to feed him the way he fed Rex. Joey could have simply let them swim around in the water and have Rex eat at his leisure, but it was more fun to toss them in the gator's mouth as he lay bathing in the sun. Sometimes

Rex wouldn't even bite down right away either, and the fish would flop around at the floor of his mouth, desperate. They were like Magikarp thrust from their Poké Balls into a strange world, desperate to metabolize oxygen or evolve their way out of danger. And they never did.

Whenever Rex swallowed, Joey held his hands under the gator's belly, feeling the food sliding along the scales like he once did with Spike. But Rex's scales were thicker, tougher, and there was so much in between them and Rex's softer insides that Joey had a hard time feeling anything at all. More often the boy nuzzled Rex's belly up against his own shirtless chest, feeling the weight of him. The warmth. Keisha was never around for Rex, but Joey wished he could show his mother how friendly his pet alligator was. He hoped that she might be proud of him for raising this creature that grew so big so fast, yet so well-behaved. Other family members stayed away from Rex. The fact of the alligator, or rather the succession of pets from guinea pigs to fire belly newts, was somehow just evidence of Joey's weird gayness, that evil lurking deep within his soul that even he didn't understand but was starting to believe in all the same. At least then he'd have something to believe in, some concrete category in which his body could definitely belong. All Joey knew was that he liked having something warm to touch, that would touch him back sometimes. No one else would look at Rex or lay a finger on him, and Joey decided that this obscurity was probably best. It was Joey and Rex, Rex and Joey against the world.

But one day, coming in from the backyard, Joey realized

that Rex could barely fit inside the old lizard cage. His body was stuck in one position, and he'd strain to turn around, his little legs struggling, and his tail pushed up against the glass. In search of a larger cage Joey went back to Birds, Birds, Birds, and the owner showed him some newer, larger options. The cheapest one would cost two hundred and ninety-nine dollars and ninety-nine cents. Hearing that figure, Joey froze up for a second.

"But I need one now," he said.

"Yeah, it's okay," the owner said, slightly confused. "Just ask your parents."

The audacity in the man's suggestion sent Joey into a rage. *How about you ask your fucking parents?* he thought. He could not stand talk of parents, the word "parents," the verb "to parent." It invited a kind of plural normalcy that he'd never been a part of and by then had started to dislike even in theory. Such innocuous comments made things real for him. Only in these moments was he forced to wonder what it might have been like to have a mommy or daddy that he could— like Kevin, that annoyingly spoiled kid around the corner—be viciously ungrateful for. He hated the contemplation of it, the mental begging for the love of an adult human, or at least the pretense of love sealed through obligation. The Birds, Birds, Birds man, and so many others without ever thinking, would force Joey into the depressive spiral of wondering what it might be like to have just one person around with the space, desire, or the strength to love a little boy who they hated for being any number of things he didn't quite understand.

But Joey knew better than to whine, especially publicly. He told himself that a lack of coddling would make him stronger. He'd be better for it in the long run. *And besides*, he thought, *other people have it worse.*

"Never mind," he said to the man. "I don't even need it."

Walking back to Paul Street, Joey thought about his mom and them, about Ganny and Mika and Tia and Popop and that little dickhead Kevin and the whole fucking block and how horrible things must have happened to her, to them, and he was right. He wanted to forgive them. The best he could do was try to hate less often. He was too good for a father who'd rape a thirteen-year-old girl, and, in fact, too good for every man and boy he'd met thus far in his ten years of life. Everyone knew Popop was fucked up, but he was definitely the only one who would give Joey and his siblings a place to live. And that mattered. The boy's anger toward the man in Birds, Birds, Birds was irrational, sickening. He'd been so nice to Joey, if only transactional. So the boy had no right to be as angry as he was with the old man for assuming he had a dependable, plural set of parents. Not just any parents, but ones who could and would dispense two hundred and ninety-nine dollars and ninety-nine cents toward a home for a giant reptile they pretended didn't exist. The whole equation, and everything stuck underneath it, was just too exhausting.

Joey returned the too-big alligator's body with no refund and no conversation. Back at home he cleaned out the cage and left it in the alleyway to be taken out with the trash. And if he didn't know better, he might have thought none of it ever even happened.

O n Paul Street, there was a family of African girls living across from Popop's apartment. One of them was in high school. People called her Erica, though Joey knew that wasn't her real name. He went along with it anyway. Her sisters, who were around Joey's age, called her something else that sounded longer and more natural to them and less natural to Joey. Erica's two little sisters, Joey thought, were annoying as hell. They always assumed he wanted to play double dutch or hopscotch with them and Mika, which he did, but he knew that they would say no, so he was always trying to act like he hadn't wanted to, to such an extent that he'd even convinced himself completely that he really didn't want to, even though they somehow still really knew he wanted to play. Whenever they saw him walk out the door, before he could even speak they'd start yelling.

"Na ah! You can't play with us!" Then they would turn to Mika. "Mika, tell your brother he can't play with us!"

Joey couldn't remember Mika replying at all. She just went on with the double dutch and shook her head, laughing. Joey was kind of jealous that she had friends like that, with whom she could communicate by saying so little. On and off, he'd try to teach Mika how to play video games with him, thinking that this would make her his friend instead. He lured her into some of his then favorites: *Streets of Rage*, *Teenage Mutant Ninja Turtles*, and especially *Golden Axe*, all of which favored cooperation. Joey would sit in front of the television screen, trying to train Mika with a focus he could never dedicate to anything else.

"Mika!" he'd yell. "What the fuck you doin? You gotta use your special move!"

Or "I know you ain't just use up the last life like that."

It was almost always the same, but sometimes he'd switch things up and beat her up in *Mortal Kombat* or *Street Fighter*. In those games, he was frustrated because she didn't provide much of a challenge.

"You a cheater," she'd say. "You only pick Sub-Zewo or Wyu. I'm tellin cause you a cheater, Joey. A damn cheater."

"No, you just corny," he'd say. "Ain't no rules about who you pick."

And Mika would sit there blank faced. Sometimes she would say sorry, and Joey would shake his head and huff and say things like *It's fine, Mika. It's fine.* Sometimes it was fine, and sometimes it wasn't. After the last time Ganny sold Joey's Sega to the pawn shop, though, on that second and penultimate occurrence, Joey stopped caring as much about winning. He blew the roach parts out of the cartridges with less fervor, assuming they'd be gone soon anyway. Assuming that after they were gone, Ganny would first lie about it then apologize, and then Popop would curse or beat her. And they were gone, and she did, and he did. It was in between Ataris, Nintendos, Segas, or PlayStations that Joey was forced outside the most. It took forever to get new ones on cutting grass outside Lustrik Corp. and his twenty-dollar allowance, mostly because he spent so much on food. Sometimes Popop bought him new gaming systems and told him to hide them from Ganny, to watch out for her, which was confusing. Where would he hide the games inside the apartment? And even if he could hide the games, he felt uncomfortable hiding things from Ganny, as if it meant that he agreed with Popop on how she was, even though he definitely didn't want his games to keep getting stolen. Whenever Popop used a credit card to buy a new system, he first spat and yelled in Joey's face, calling him a bitch and ungrateful and a faggot, which made it a little more difficult to enjoy the thing at hand. *At least*, he thought, *Ganny eventually apologized for stealing them in the first place.*

Joey was most annoyed with Erica's little sisters during these times, when there was yelling or fighting in the apartment and no games to play. From the steps he watched them all play Patty Cake, seething because he did, in fact, want to play that game. Maybe it was the hands and the touching. He remembered that it felt good to touch people, especially girls, but Prudy was gone and his aunt Tia was becoming distant.

By the time he got to middle school, she wouldn't even kiss or hump anymore at all. Looking out of the window all summer, Joey wondered if both the girls' and Tia's distancing from him had anything to do with the fact that he'd grown in wrong, like a painful toenail. Maybe he was too big, but not the right kind of big, a kind of big unsuitable for the type of touching he wanted. His titties flattened out, and he still had a bird chest, just not as much. Did anyone even notice these minor adjustments? He was much taller and skinnier than everyone his age, *like a spaghetti noodle*, some said. People called him the names of different cartoon skeletons so he always kept his shirt on even when other boys didn't. And his teeth were still a problem, his head was still rather large, and his ears too small. From afar, with his mouth closed, he looked kind of like a thin, armless tree holding up the Egg of the King. Hair always nappy, too. Old ladies on his street would say, *Why is that boy hair so peezy? Who is your mother? She let you go out the house like that?* It was hard to tell what the problem was from his own perspective, let alone what other people saw as his problem; then there was the whole separate matter of what might actually be wrong.

Joey appreciated that the African girls across the street never teased him. He did not appreciate the fact that they would not let him play Patty Cake. Their older sister, Erica, was a little different. She was too cool for most of the kids because she was even older than Tia. And Erica looked like a grown woman, really tall and dark with big thighs and other body parts. She had a gap, too, and in this, Joey must have thought they were kindred spirits. Erica wasn't quite friends with Tia, either, but they knew each other, frenemies perhaps. Behind Erica's back, Tia would make jokes that Joey thought were mean, but he laughed anyway. He felt giddy and conspiratorial as Tia called Erica "the African Booty Scratcher" or "That Amazon Chick Across the Street." Joey preferred the name Amazon Chick, though, because he first mistook it for a compliment. He was obsessed with going to the Amazon one day, lifting up rocks, and putting his head inside of tree trunks to find bats and snakes and bright-colored frogs. And, of course, Joey still thought Erica was really pretty, even though Tia would say things like "That bitch don't even do her hair. Dumb ass ponytail," which was weird, Joey thought, because his aunt Tia and Mika and them used to rock that same ponytail sometimes too.

For Joey, Erica was a woman, unlike any he'd seen in real life. Keisha was sick, or high or gone, not a woman. And Ganny was Ganny, not a woman. His teachers were white ladies who felt more robot than human. And Mika and Tia were girls. A little girl and a big girl. Besides, Erica might have actually been somewhere other than where Joey had always been, where he would always be, right there on Paul Street. She sounded stronger and smarter too. Her voice, even though she barely spoke, both excited and intimidated him. She never spoke to him directly, but would glance at him from the corner of her eye when replying to someone else, maybe because they were always the two tallest people. And Joey hung on every word: Algebra, Africa, Art, Science. To other people, she never seemed to be saying anything special, but to

Joey these were new words, new spaces never uttered by any-body in his apartment. From behind her glasses, Erica seemed bored saying these things, but Joey had all these questions. For one, where the hell was Africa? What does it look like? How do you do science? Is science something like alchemy? Was algebra, then, like adding and subtracting? He never wanted her to stop talking, even if it wasn't to him. Even the high school Erica went to was farther away than Joey could imagine, in the deep Northeast where everybody had houses. It had to be better. As far as the boy could tell, Erica was the most educated person he'd ever met. And that was something that felt important to be someday. Educated. He knew being educated was important because it was the very thing that everyone else he knew was not, and had no interest in.

Erica wasn't normally outside with the younger kids, but sometimes she was. When the fire hydrant was on, she wore one-piece bathing suits while everybody else wore shorts and T-shirts. Some nights, Erica would stay out late and play games with everyone, like Spin the Bottle. Mika and her friends were either not allowed or disinterested in those games. Tia would tell her she was too little and send her back inside. In such moments Tia's authority excited Joey. It made him feel like part of some inner circle by proxy, the VP of all the big-kid nighttime games. Tia was tiny, but everybody knew she was older and knew things, so they deferred to her, especially in matters of mischief. Still frustrating, though, was the fact that outside, Tia never let Joey touch her, and she never touched him when other people were around. She acted colder and more distant, which made Joey unsure if he was doing something wrong, or if what they did together sometimes would look wrong to other people. Erica's presence made it easier for Joey to think otherwise.

But there was also this buck-toothed light-skin boy hanging around all the time that Joey hated. Kevin. Always in the way. Kevin had an egghead like Joey's too, and it was infuriating when people would mention the two of them in the same sentence. Adults considered them friends, but Joey felt no guilt about wishing Kevin dead. That spoiled bastard Kevin. From what Joey could gather, he lived in a whole house just a few blocks away with no roaches and two parents that hugged him every day after school, but he was always complaining about it. How far Kevin had to walk to get there for Spin the Bottle, how Kevin's mommy—he always said it like that, "mommy"—had made eggplant lasagna and he didn't like it, but she made him eat it all, or how he had to clean his room, the whole room he had to himself. *Fuck Kevin*, Joey thought, being sure not to make eye contact with the other boy ever, lest he betray the desire for violence. Sometimes Joey couldn't even focus on the game at hand with Kevin around. The worst part was that for some reason, everyone felt bad for Kevin because he paraded around like he was hard, had stories of that rough life he was living and all its perils, so girls thought he was cool and most of the boys were afraid of him; teachers thought he just needed special attention, which they were only too eager to provide. *That dickhead Kevin*, Joey thought. *What I wouldn't do to get rid of him.* Meanwhile, Kevin sat perfectly calm in his clean clothes and new Jordans while Joey seethed at him with all the other kids oblivious, gathered around an empty 40 oz of Colt 45 watching the bottle spin.

Joey knew it was difficult to cheat, technically, when playing Spin the Bottle, but that didn't change his suspicions about Kevin. In Joey's opinion, not a single pair of lips should ever touch anywhere on Kevin's face or body, not even his mommy's. Kevin with his clean Speed Racer T-shirts and fresh Nikes, Kevin with his crisp haircuts and beady little rat eyes. Joey was afraid of what might happen if Kevin understood how deeply he was hated. That spoiled little brat. That child who seemed to be the locus of so much affection and turned out somehow, some way, to still be an utter dickhead despite everything. Joey couldn't help wondering, constantly, what he might do if approached with the kind of love that he swore to death Kevin was getting. It was good then, that Spin the Bottle was short-lived. Watching Kevin kiss Tia or Erica made Joey gag. The kissing altogether—lip pecks and even the tongue stuff—got boring fast for a group of would-be adolescents that had long since been treated like adults. There were other more exciting games to be had. Tia introduced them all to a game called Catch a Girl Fuck a Girl, which most of the other kids called Catch a Girl Freak a Girl because not everybody was as comfortable with profanity as Tia was. Joey, though, said "fuck" every chance he could get, not just making a point about his boldness but his age. He had adult written all over him. *Fuck Stearne Elementary*, Joey thought, *and all the grimey ass kids who go there. Fuck Popop, too, and fuck roaches, fuck food stamp cereal, fuck this, fuck that, etc.*

But Joey never said "fuck" about Catch a Girl Fuck a Girl. One of the best parts was that Kevin couldn't run fast. At all. He was like a little box turtle. Joey was Bugs Bunny. A master runner, if ever there was one. Once, when Keisha was trying to beat him with a broom because he complained that she was doing crack too much, he literally smoked her; he bolted so fast from her grip that she fell to the floor trying to hold on, old powder from the carpet billowing up in the living room. Mika laughed and got popped on the hand. And, of course, Joey got his ass whooped later, but still, in that brief moment of escape, he was proud. Just for a moment. To run with purpose, in a way that allowed him to finally catch his own breath, was something to be proud of.

The girls got a head start, but that didn't matter. Joey predicted where everyone would run. He had practice from Freeze Tag and free ball with all the neighborhood boys whenever they didn't have enough people to play without him. He couldn't beat any one of them in a fight, or tackle them, or take a hit, but he could run. Faster than all. He figured this was why they hit him so hard when they caught up, for making them work. Now, chasing after the girls was no problem. He bolted after Erica, who ran toward his elementary school. The sun hadn't gone all the way down yet and was straddling the iron fences of the schoolyard, the Baptist church, and Lustrik Corp. down the road. Erica and Joey ran past reluctant boys and girls on Paul Street, past the Post Office on their right and that house with the lady who had like eleven scary eggheaded sons on their left, past the house with two German shepherds and the auto garage with odd hours, past the white lady's house who called everybody who looked scruffy a nigger no matter what color they were, and right up to the Stearne Elementary schoolyard fence.

Realizing there was no one else around, Erica slowed a little. She looked back at Joey, smiling. Then she stopped completely, with both hands on her hips.

"Okay. You caught me," she said. "What you gone do?"

It was a good question. Joey hadn't written anything down. He had received little, if any, verbal instruction. With Tia, it was mostly moving bodies in ways that made things wetter as opposed to more dry, or nudging his head. He'd never been asked to explain it before, and now it seemed especially impossible, even though his winkey was already hard, just thinking about it. Saying to Erica "I wanna do it" out loud just felt dumb. Would he say, *I wanna do it with you?* Of course not; he shook off the thought. What was *it*, really, anyway? Joey stood there with his mouth open as if he was preparing to say something, trying to stall. He wanted to say, *Can I ask Tia and then come back?*

Erica didn't wait for Joey's reply. She grabbed his hand, which felt so good, oh so good to be wanted in that way, and led him into the locked schoolyard through the hole in the fence. They went straight to the corner of the yard. Just by the ramp where Joey bought fifty-cent soft pretzels on Wednesdays. There was a grate in the ground. Beneath it, a dry concrete space with one door that was always locked. To Joey, the space felt six feet deep. It had to be six feet deep. And once you jumped down and closed the grate afterward, no one could really tell you were in there from the outside. Being down there made you invisible to the whole world. The boy had never actually hopped in before, afraid of heights as he was, so skittish with risk, but Erica jumped down first and helped him. As soon as his sneakers touched the bottom, Erica took her shirt off and unbuttoned her blue jeans.

Erica's titties were bigger than the ones he'd seen on HBO After Dark and sat at such a height that Joey could lick them standing up. The hole they were in smelled like pee, but it didn't matter. Joey's winkey was the hardest it had ever been. It was strange, though, because everything felt so serious. Tia and Joey would rub or lick on each other with and without clothes, but that was in a bed. And they were mostly just touching. It felt like playing, especially when Joey's clothes were on, even if he was licking Tia's coochie or titties. With the woman beneath the grate, it was both more exciting and scarier; the stakes were so much higher. He had to perform now, and do something new, take some next step that was always just being alluded to. And this might be his only chance to do it, sweaty palms and headache and all. Both Joey's mom and Popop had told him—at this one miraculous point in which they both agreed—that if he didn't do it right, the girl would never talk to him again, and such a thought, now that he and Erica were ready to plan their lives together, was terrifying. Joey felt like he might not be able to do it right. He was afraid that he wasn't doing it right before, and that was why Tia didn't really want him anymore, let alone when they were outside. *That must be why*, he would think as they got older, as she started having him watch her bike while she went into her boyfriend's house. And what did doing it right really mean? Sure, you're supposed to eat the coochie, everybody knew that. But like, what else? Joey supposed that Erica would guide things because she was bigger and smarter and had done it before. While Joey was wasting time thinking, Erica had taken off all her clothes except her big glasses and blue-and-white-striped Adidas.

She laughed at him impatiently. "You gone take ya clothes off?"

Joey laughed too, removing his blue velour FILA pants. He didn't want to take off his shirt and have Erica laugh at his chest. *There will be time, though*, he thought. Later on in their relationship, after he'd gotten stronger, he would walk around the house bare chested looking out at mountains, the same ones people would later use as screensavers, through large glass windows in their living room, stretching and flexing and saying things other people in movies said with ease, like "Good morning, honey. I love you," and "What would you like to do today?"

When his pants came off, Erica reached out for Joey's winkey. Her hands were big and soft and warm playing with it. She brought the hand back to her coochie and then to Joey's winkey again and it was wetter and warmer. Joey wondered if this was a good time to ask about their plans for the future, to tell her about all the meals he had made in the Easy-Bake Oven, how he could cook for them, to tell her that he planned to get emancipated from his family soon and they could move into a house somewhere far away when he got a job. But how might he explain that she would need to have a job, too, because he didn't play that freeloading shit? With one hand still sliding up and down Joey's winkey, Erica turned around and rubbed her butt against him. Joey could feel the wetness of her coochie around his waist before he even touched it; he angled his waist up a little bit because her legs were longer. She touched herself and then him again so it was wet and felt a little too good, like something he didn't deserve. *The best he will ever feel*, he thought. And then, while she was guiding him into her, the boy felt a tingling sensation. He was just about to do it and the tingling took over; his hands were shaking and he squeezed onto Erica's butt real tight. Her hand on his winkey slowed down a little. It felt like something was coming out of him as he trembled, but there was just a little bit of clear fluid at the end. It was impossible for Joey to think about anything bad at that moment. It was like he didn't have to be part of the world anymore.

"Are you gone put it in?" Erica said. But Joey's eyes were closed and the tingling had his whole body clenched, seizing him, particularly his legs, which wobbled a little. He couldn't hear anything but a ringing in his ears, his waist tight against Erica's butt, his hands clasping on to her for dear life.

Then, nothing.

"What you doin?" Erica said. She seemed frustrated. Joey

didn't know what he was doing or what he should do, so when the tingling was over he dry-humped Erica's butt. "Is you gonna put it in?" she repeated slowly, and overly correct. Then she reached back and felt that Joey's winkey wasn't hard anymore.

"Did you fuckin cum?" she said. It was a new word for the boy, but he figured through syntax that she was talking about the tingling. The tingling was everything. It was something to aspire to, but not judging by Erica's face, scowling and confused. Joey figured that Erica wanted the tingling, too. He knew that girls could get it if you ate the coochie right, and imagined it would be the same way with a woman like Erica. He had a plan. He started to explain it.

"I can—"

But then Erica cut him off with a slap. "I can't believe you fuckin came," she said. "Not in me, right?" She mumbled a little more, putting her clothes on. "What the fuck."

"I'm sorry," Joey said, rubbing his cheek. "We can just stay here, though."

Erica sucked her teeth. "You *is* a lil faggot," she said, fixing her bra. Before Joey could say anything else she extended her palm to his face. "Don't talk to me."

Joey started pulling his pants up because he didn't know what else to do. He could ask Tia for advice, hoping she wouldn't get mad, or he could come up with a plan to make Erica stay in the hole with him. Joey knew his winkey would get hard again, and soon. And maybe then he could do something. If only he had a second chance, he would get it right. He

was a fast learner. Everybody said so. He just needed something that would make Erica want to sleep over with him, go
with him, hug him at night before bed. Anything. He shook
as it all faded away: the house, the dog, the black wrought
iron fence behind which two emus, a serval cat, and an Irish
wolfhound would greet the neighbors in their unusually safe
neighborhood as the kids frolicked and giggled and danced
in the sprinklers, ignoring all the touching and sucking and
licking and feeling and pure warmness going on between him
and Erica all day long on the inside.

"Wait," Joey said, stalling, but trying not to scare her.

"Fuck outta here," Erica said. "You a little ass boy." And
she pushed up the grate on her tippy-toes and climbed out.

Tia or some of the other kids must have seen Erica leaving
the hole because they showed up so quick after she left. It was
dark and Tia stood over the grate alone.

"Smell like padussy down there," she said, smiling and
helping Joey climb out. "Let me find out you done got you
some."

Joey straightened himself out a little, being sure to avoid
looking Tia in the face. "Yeah," he said. "I think she wanna
go together."

"Yeeaah," Tia said. "That's my lil tall ass nigga."

SOME SUMMERS

some summers Tia and Joey went on adventures. They listened to Linkin Park, Chevelle, and Slipknot riding down too-steep hills on Dyno trick bikes with pegs on the front and back. They stopped at basketball courts listening to Beenie Man and Sean Paul, played two-on-two with older boys who were always trying to fuck Tia, and stole, maybe for the last time one summer, that last time they might be mistaken for children, snacks and toys from Kmart. All through Frankford and Mayfair and the Greater Northeast, they dug up dirt. They played knock knock zoom zoom where white folks owned houses and trimmed hedges and, whenever the knocking and the zooming wasn't quick enough, answered the door with shotguns for those pesky kids. Everybody was escalating. It made Joey and Tia laugh; they could hit harder, run faster, lust more deeply but probably never again for each other. They jumped, wantonly, from *second- and third-story* balconies playing tag, just to show off. It was easy, their arms flailing for years before hitting the ground and rolling. They were unstoppable in the summer. Uncatchable.

Popop stayed home boiling blue crabs in malt liquor and hot sauce, glowing orbs of red seasoning that came in little plastic baggies and enough garlic to melt every single one of the Lost Boys. The old man played Caps out front with neighborhood kids, and all of a sudden it was safe for Joey to play, too; was he getting too big, too unfuckwithable, or was Popop getting too old, too tired? Together, they loaded Ragu and Snapple lids with Play-Doh, sliding them across the concrete thunder dome in the middle of the street, rainbow chalk marking the limits of wins and losses, cursing for fun.

"Fuck outta here, cutty. You think you good now?"

Or, "Damn, cutty, how you let ya grandson bust ya ass like that?"

"Oh, I taught that little nigga. He learned all that from me."

And after an L, Popop might check on the crabs, Joey's mouth just watering all the time like a *Lion King* hyena. A live crab might pop up in the street, mouth all foamy and clamping onto a bottle cap, the whole neighborhood laughing at the crab's struggle to be somebody.

"I bet you can't even beat this crab," somebody said.

"Nigga, you look like this crab," Joey said.

People laughed.

Joey and Tia took off again. To pet shops, farther ones than Birds, Birds, Birds this time, deeper down Frankford Ave, on corners where the magic shop used to be, outside Frankford Hospital where they once adjusted Joey's broken pinky finger.

They left their bikes outside to stare at bearded dragons and hamsters. *What is the real difference between a guinea pig and a hamster? And if they eat the same thing, doesn't that make them the same basic kind of animal? Can they live in the same cage together? Is it bad to want them to live in a cage at all?* They were showing signs of aging. At a new pet shop between Bridge and Pratt, Joey got his bike stolen while he was inside snuggling brown and white gerbils. He came out, yelling a performance for Tia, *Fuck outta here, bitch niggas! Better run!* glad the thieves had already gone so there would be no fighting. He rode on Tia's back pegs, and sometimes Tia rode on his. If it was still warm by September, they cut school. Joey waited outside while Tia visited older boys in houses under the El, peeking through the windows and listening through the door, growing hard and jealous at the sounds their bodies made against each other.

At night, they climbed railroad tracks, hog-spit on rocks, and pelted cars with boulders. Unbearable adrenaline. Windshields cracked, shattered, and splashed under their whole-body throws. It set Joey on fire. Cars crashed into light poles and corner stores, erupting into flame, causing alarm and chaos and joy.

"That was a good shot," Tia might say.

And Joey would grab another rock. Faster. Competing with Tia, who grabbed three. Another windshield smashed.

"You fucked that one up," Joey said.

He imagined the startled driver, struck out of the comfort of his AC as the car twisted off the road. He could not stop throwing and being happy. Someone yelled from down below. The kids ran. Little black lightning bolts.

"Race you home," Joey said.

And Tia was the only one who could match his speed. People said what they wanted about Joey, but he could run. He ran from everything. Tia never said what she was running from, or why she was living with her dad, or where her mom was now, but she ran just as hard.

One Saturday afternoon, Mika ran into the house crying louder than Joey had ever heard. Popop was home and annoyed instantly. She was interrupting his football game. A stack of pink pools clutched in his left hand, he was yelling and standing and sitting and with no one but himself. He held a 40 oz in his other hand and would pause periodically, looking at the pools, circling and crossing things out. Joey was playing *Azure Dreams*, really fucking things up in the tower with his baby dragon, impressing all the neighborhood NPC girls. He just could never collect enough creature eggs; he liked watching them hatch, every one of them a new opportunity for greatness. Being a collector of living things had come so naturally. Sometimes he named the creatures after Pokémon or Digimon even though none of the townspeople understood his subtle and not-so-subtle intertextual engagements. NPCs were just like that, it seemed. And there were so many damned NPCs, whether they knew it or not. When

Joey had opened the PlayStation on Christmas, Popop said, *You better fuckin appreciate this shit. Shit cost a lot of money.* And that was exactly what Joey was doing that moment when his sister ran into the apartment crying. But Popop didn't really like that, either. He'd always yell at Joey, and sometimes Jeremy, to get up and go outside, while they read subtitles and dialogue to each other, unraveling story as best they could. But on this particular day, when Mika came in crying, Joey was alone with Popop, each segregated to their own screens. Julian was there in a corner, migrating between babbles and being completely frozen like some kind of odd commercial toddler thing.

Mika, clutching her left cheek and standing blank inside the doorway, kept yelling, "He hit me! He hit me!"

Joey tried to act like nothing had happened. But Popop, enraged that anyone would have hit his little girl, slammed his Old English down on the table and turned toward the door. "Who?" he said. "Who the what the fuck you talkin bout, Mika, and stop cryin. Spit that shit out and stop cryin, what happened?"

"Kevin! He hit me!" Mika yelled again. She was sobbing so deeply that she had to force the yell out. Otherwise, it would have been hard to understand her. "He slapped me. And he called me a bitch cause I don't wanna kiss him."

Shit, Joey thought. This could not be ignored.

"Where that little nigga at?" Popop said, glancing at Joey and then the door. He turned back to his grandson before Mika could answer. "Go find his little ass, Joey. Go make yaself useful. If you let one of these niggas fuck wit ya sister and you don't do nothin, imma beat ya little faggot ass."

"Outside," Mika said, stuttering, pointing.

Joey took a deep breath. He wondered if this was how things started with Keisha or Ganny, if boys had started hitting them and making them cry at this age. Was it someone like Popop who had to stand up for them? And even more strange, was the complete inversion of this dynamic where once they were grown it was okay to hit them yourself? At least Joey was at a save point in *Azure Dreams*; no matter what happened he would have something to look forward to later. As long as he survived. But he was conflicted. He would love to see Kevin dead, of course, but he was no executioner. He'd never even tried to hurt someone physically like that before. Such a late bloomer. The furthest he'd gotten was pushing Mika off some video game she broke or throwing pillows at her. And even then, Popop popped him on the head and demanded that he let her play, too. When she sat on and smothered a kitten he'd found, Joey took the light bulb out of the basement and locked her down there. Sometimes he tried to tell scary stories at night to make her cry when she bought into the lies their mother told. Some of those stories were about Keisha never coming back to get them because she was a crackhead. Joey had pushed and teased Mika in most every way that was not punching or slapping or beating her with a weapon. This felt like an achievement.

Joey wanted to love his little sister, but knew that saying it unabashedly, to her especially, would make them both weaker.

Or he would appear weaker, and she would just start calling him a faggot, too. With the slightest shift in power, she might turn from little sister to archnemesis. She was adorable but needed to grow up faster just like he did. And here she was, wailing right through the carefully curated silence. When she came in crying, her hair was in two big pony puffs with purple barrettes. By then, Mika was chunky and darker-skinned than him. It was said that her dad, unlike Joey's, was, without a doubt, black. This made her unquestionably black and irrefutable when she teamed up with Tia or Popop or Keisha to say that Joey was a sissy white boy. But that wasn't what put Joey most at odds with her. It was the fact that she could receive tenderness, that she was allowed to. It was the shared idea that she was a child both deserving of and in need of kindness. The house responded to her in ways that it did not to him. Anytime, at her age and younger, when Joey came in the house crying because he got jumped or his nose was broken because he was kicked and spit on and hit with shit, it would only mean more beatings. And cursing. But for Mika, all it took was one slap from Kevin, and Popop was ready to murder.

It hurt to think about.

But she was smaller than him, and a girl, so she was weaker, and that was just how it was. The outside world would be harder for her than for him, if they ever got there. And did this make her more deserving of familial love? But Tia was a girl, too, and smaller than him but stronger and smarter than he and Mika combined. *So then why is it so much different?* Joey thought. Why couldn't someone defend him like this?

Because Joey was jealous of Mika, that people were sometimes nice to her, he hated to admit how much he enjoyed her voice despite her nauseating optimism. He liked the way she smiled when he patted her on the head, that she was afraid of things that he should have been afraid of too, that she let him practice that rolling throw that Ryu did in *Street Fighter*, even emerging from the throw closet giggling after each landing in a pile of clothes that fit neither of them. He abused the fact that they were more likely to get food when she asked for it, even though she never said she was hungry. And despite being bitter about the kitten, he knew it was an accident. He would have groomed that calico street cat to eat the faces and suck the souls of his enemies; it was gonna be just like that movie *Sleepwalkers*. A SWAT Kat, if nothing else, a fucking menace to society, a grown-up, humanoid, technologically advanced and skinless face-eating beast.

But it died.

After Mika sat on it. And he called her fatty fatty fat fat and fuzzy lumpkins, and she cut him on the arm with a kitchen knife, which resulted in Joey getting stitches and a beating, but the cat was still dead.

And he couldn't escape these thoughts as he took his time pausing the PlayStation and putting his sneakers on. Mika was still crying, but staring at *him* now. Even she knew what had to be done. Joey had an obligation. Not to Popop, but to his little sister, to provide her with tenderness through violence. The boy was vaguely aware by then that in a normal, structured family like the ones on television, older siblings were supposed to protect younger ones. Especially older boys. It was a rule. He stepped out of the apartment door and into the hallway with his chest up as high as he could get it. Joey's whole body was balled up in anger, fists clenched at whatever. He pushed away any concept of peaceful resolution. Then he walked past the second door in the hallway, past the mailboxes on his right, and down the three concrete steps leading out onto Paul Street. Kevin was outside, just standing there like nothing had happened. As if both what he did ten minutes ago and what Joey was thinking were perfectly normal and impossible to question.

"Hey, Kevin," Joey said. "You wanna come play the game?" Not once had Joey ever asked Kevin to play any game, because he hated him. But Kevin was dumb, so he didn't know that. For some reason, he thought the two boys were friends. *Relationships*, Joey thought, *are so shallow that most people can't even tell whether the person likes or despises them, and that is more sad than being by yourself.* Joey had, of course, always played down his hatred to avoid confrontation, even when Kevin spit on him to show some other boys how cool he was. This sacrifice to avoid such a confrontation had worked out so well, though. Until now.

"Yeah," Kevin said, jogging up to the apartment door. "What games you got?"

Joey turned to walk back inside with Kevin following, then he stopped at the mailboxes, anxious to hurt someone. As soon as they were both into the hallway, Joey stopped and turned to Kevin. "What you do to my sister?" he asked.

"Nothin, what you mean?" Kevin said.

"Kevin, why you hit my little sister?" Joey said.

"Man, I ain't do nothin to her. She bein a punk. I was just play—"

And then Joey interrupted Kevin with his fist. He had his thumb on the outside, like Popop always taught him. His knuckles landed flat on Kevin's cheek. It was so soft. Kevin's head slammed into the silver mailboxes nailed against the wall; their hollow sound rang out through the short hallway; one of them even flew open. Kevin clutched his cheek. It was bright red. Mika heard the sound and ran out into the hall. Popop was behind her. Joey just stood there watching Kevin fold inside of himself. He looked back and forth between the other boy's face and his own fist, aching.

"Fuck happenin out here?" Popop said, bursting out of the apartment door. He turned to Kevin. "Kevin, you fuckin call my granddaughter a bitch?"

Kevin started crying way too loud and ran away. Then Joey, confused all of a sudden, even though everything had gone according to plan, scurried into the apartment like a roach under the frigerator. He sat on the couch feeling brolic and strange and dizzy holding back tears, looking at his fist, swelling and hurting, and clutching one hand in the other. He couldn't believe how much it hurt, how quickly any feeling of achievement had vanished, if it had even appeared to begin with. How could winning make him feel like less of a person? Or worse than getting beaten up? Maybe Joey didn't hit him hard enough to feel what he was supposed to feel, that intoxicating feeling that so many boys seemed to revel in each and every day. It was only his first time punching someone in the face after all, and there was so much he didn't know yet; perhaps he would just have to get used to it.

Mika sat next to him on the couch, dead silent. Popop was back in front of the game like nothing ever happened.

Ganny, stirring awake from the noise, walked into the living room groggy. "What yall doin out there?" she said.

"Bitch," Popop said, "can yall just shut the fuck up? I'm watchin the game, damn." He turned up the volume on the TV.

Ganny walked up to the kids and stood over them, staring down.

"What happened to ya hand?" she asked Joey.

He whispered to her, "Nothin, Ganny. I'm hungry, though."

"Me too," said Mika.

"Aight, aight, imma make some food, damn, calm down," Ganny said, before turning toward the kitchen. Then she stopped to frown at Joey. "Why you holdin ya hand like that then?"

"I hit it by accident," Joey said. But he felt so much shame, and it wasn't because of the lie. He supposed that maybe he was ashamed of punching someone in the face, stooping to that level, or maybe it wasn't that simple. He didn't know if the shame was based on why he did it, or the fact that for a brief moment, it might have felt good to let his fist go.

"Yeah, okay" was all Ganny said.

And Joey sat there on the couch next to Mika, squishing

and sliding and sweaty in the plastic. Then Ganny came back with a bag full of ice for his hand. He took it, and without saying a word, she returned to the kitchen.

Joey turned the game back on, but didn't wipe the tears coming down his face. Mika watched him breathing. He didn't turn to her, but watched her out the corner of one eye.

"Thank you, Joey," she said.

The ice was slipping from his knuckles, melting all over the place.

"Don't cry," Mika went on. "It's okay." And she patted her older brother on the shoulder.

But Popop heard this and said he shouldn't be crying like a little bitch anyway, and if he didn't stop, he would hit Joey himself. Joey did his best then to shift the crying into deep breathing. In and out. And shivering. In and out.

THE STARS, THE OCEAN, THE BOYS

In *Star Ocean: The Second Story*, a boy named Claude Kenny lands on an underdeveloped (third world?) planet called Expel. Stranded in a lush rainforest with bioluminescent caves and dysmorphic animals, he runs into Rena, a native Expellian, all blue hair and long ears. Rena is being attacked by a mutant gorilla, a tiny replica of King Kong—or maybe a rabid Saiyan prince struck dumb by the moon. But just before she gets mauled, Claude jumps in to save her with his blond bob. You, the player, are Claude. You have, in your brown bomber jacket, a gun. A Photon Blaster, more precisely, on a planet where people do not yet understand evolution. The ray of light coming from your weapon makes you seem like a god, dispatching the gorilla in one shot with 499 damage, which, you will soon discover, is a lot at level 1. Rena is certain that you are a hero from prophecy, the Warrior of Light, sent to save Expel from the Sorcery Globe: a meteor that crash-landed there and has caused anomalies like super-powered gorillas attacking blue-haired women in forests, and what seem to be demons emerging out of thin air, the earth, people's homes, etc., like in *Diablo*. From there, your hero's quest begins.

Rena has an older brother named Dias Flac. A swordsman with long blue hair who your friend Jeremy has a crush on. He is less trustful of you, talks a ton of shit about everyone, and wears fancy pants on which he carries a thin sword like Griffith's. The difference between, say, Dias and Griffith, and even Goku, too, is Dias's selfishness. While Griffith and Goku are ready to die at any moment to save their friends and kin, Dias lifts his blade only for Rena, who, honestly, since she becomes the most powerful mage on the planet, doesn't really need his help. Nevertheless, Jeremy thinks Dias is the true god in *Star Ocean*, while you find him annoying and lazy.

You two believe in little outside of *Star Wars* or vampires, right or wrong. But together you pore hours into *Star Ocean: The Second Story*. For better or worse, you both wish for another tale, a host of second chances and righted wrongs, lusting after new endings despite the continual pain of starting over; you relish the hundred and twenty hours it takes to sweep through both the game's discs. *There has to be some way that Gabriel can survive! Claude and Dias can be friends, I know they can!* In every town you pause for private actions, splitting up the party for little chats, forcing them to mingle and get to know each other, building friendships and rivalries in every major metropolitan area.

You meet Ashton Anchors. Ashton is essentially the shit. He makes Claude and Dias look like children. Possessed by a two-headed dragon named Gyoro and Ururun, Ashton is the symbiotic hope of this new world. What had happened was, Ashton tried to vanquish the dragon, for fame, money, etc. But rather than be defeated, they decide to possess him, so now, and forever after, Ashton wanders around Expel with his dual knives and one blue and one red dragon looming over his shoulders, scrapping with each other, arguing with him, scaring people, lending him power. Lending you power. They don't look like dragons at all, really, but like snakes, like Spike and her babies, like the sea creatures you used to draw on loose-leaf paper and in the Death Note, Ashton's insides as the ocean hiding the dragon's guts. They're cute. They are your very own nine-tails fox; you are Expel's official jinchuriki. First thought of as a curse, yall learn to love Gyoro and Ururun, cuddling and coddling them, dependent on each other in an eternal three-way. Yall forget about Claude and Dias and moms smoking crack right next to you, stomachs growling, the school and neighborhood and home bullies lurking around every corner.

But there are lies. Expellians are not really Expellians.

About eighty hours into the game you learn that there are hundreds of inhabited worlds, some created, others born, from which your party of twelve heroes draws breath. You are insignificant in the grand scheme of things. Misfits, all of you: three eyes, guns, swords, magic, neurosis, carnal desire, and generalized loneliness. There is always a new enemy: Energy Nede's Ten Wise Men. It was them. *Them shady niggas*, you almost say, who created the Sorcery Globe and dropped it on Expel like that meteor near the Yucatán that killed all the dinosaurs. Indalecio leads them, and this is all his will. You and your crew must dispatch Indalecio and his friends eventually, though not without trepidation. After some high drama infighting among the Ten Wise Men, Your Own Party, Energy Nede resource management, problematic intergalactic politics, the destruction of Expel, and Claude Kenny's shitty dad getting in the way, you murder Indalecio in what comes to feel like cold blood, as he cries about inflicting all that pain in an attempt to get his daughter back.

Sitting with your legs crossed in front of the TV, you learn college-level English reading about how all this shit went down. Indalecio's daughter looks like Rena, and she stays dead with your help. So many dead bodies after a hundred and twenty hours learning cool moves and backstories and making friendships and trying to find all the different endings. And to this day, you've yet to unlock them all.

Whenever Keisha was home, she used the bathroom a lot. Whatever happened in there, Joey could never forget the smell it produced, like sour milk and burned chemicals roiling around in an old pot. *She must be an accomplice to Gargamel*, he thought, lusting after juicy little Smurfs and dreaming of one day dropping their tiny bodies into a sulfuric brew. But Smurfs weren't real; the boy speculated on what his mother put in her pot. She always swore by her cooking skills, but it was scary when she entered the kitchen: burned proteins and disappointment lingered. *Maybe she practicin in there*, a smaller Mika would say. And the facade of cooking well was Keisha's pride, and like many permanent lies, it grew into truth depending on the speaker and listener.

But there were clues. Whenever Keisha emerged from the bathroom she was bug-eyed and startled. She would say *uh-uh* and *They comin to get me* over and over again. Six- and seven- and eight- and nine-year-old Joey felt like he needed to do something about it. He needed to find out who they were and stop them from getting his mother. He needed to help her or to fix her, which, to him, were the same thing. She was like a broken machine jerking its way around the house. He thought she was dying or turning into a zombie, which were definitely not the same thing. When she walked out of the bathroom, stiff and sweating, her right hand behind her head and left hand clutching her elbow, Joey would try and pull her apart. Her limbs magnetized to her body. Joey, big for nothing, could only drown in guilt, a disappointment to himself, his mother, and his little sister as he watched the woman who gave birth to them breathe deep, in and out, and pace around the apartment.

He might grow into someone useful. Later. It wouldn't be that long, his mother always said. *You need to grow up. Get a job, boy, I can't hold you.* Old age would sneak up on him quick. It had already gotten his aunt Tia. By the time Tia was thirteen, Joey would imagine his aunt having their baby and moving away somewhere together. He wanted to speak to his mother about all these things, but he could not. Having failed to pull her apart or out of her spell, Joey resorted to hugging her whenever she entered that chemical trance. She paced around the apartment sweating, trembling, and dragging the boy as his wrapped arms sank farther down her glistening brown body.

"Mommy," he said, "what's wrong? Why you actin like that?"

She repeated his name over and over again. "Joey, wait.

Joey, just wait, goddammit wait. Just you fuckin wait," she said. "Yall gonna get what's comin."

It took a long time for Joey to figure out what was coming, but he was always anticipating it. Sometimes Keisha screamed at random. Trembling, sweating, with her left palm on her face, peering out of all the windows, opening and closing them. She dragged Joey behind her. "Stop bein a little sissy," she said, swatting at him as he tried to hold on.

When Popop was home, the older man flagged her off and called her a crackhead bitch. She was mostly invisible or annoying to him until she bumped into his body or otherwise tried to invade his privacy. Whenever she knocked on his door in such a state or brought a man home in secret to have sex for money, Popop would kick her out for a day or two. Once, she brought an old white man into the apartment while Joey was home. It was a school day, so she hadn't expected him, but the boy had already given up on elementary. The white man smiled at Joey, and he started to die from the inside out. He kept dying as Keisha told him to go in the other room and be quiet while she licked the white man's winkey on the couch. It was the first white winkey Joey had ever seen, the first other than Popop's at all. It looked lazy, as if it spent a lot of time sleeping and did not work very hard. Even though Keisha told Joey to go into the other room, there was no door, so he poked his head out and watched the whole time, the back of his mother's head and the white man's glee. When Popop found out, he made Keisha leave and delivered some body shots to Joey. Then Keisha gave him a weak beating for snitching.

Sometimes Keisha would beat Joey for asking her the wrong questions, especially if she was sweating, trembling.

"You know what. Take ya clothes off and get in the damn shower," Keisha said. It made Joey feel stupid in the beginning because he would actually take everything off and start rinsing himself, mostly with just water. Confused. He rarely used soap if there was soap. No one really used the shower except Tia, who took her own things in and out with her. The tile was dry and brown. Being told by Keisha to get in the shower made Joey feel like she cared, like she was worried about him. He thought that if there was any grown-up he could eventually trust, it would be Keisha. Should be Keisha. Her beatings were a comparative gift. She couldn't hit as hard as Popop and would tire quickly. By the time Joey was in middle school, she could hardly pierce his flesh. He could trust her.

"She ya mom," people would say.

"Mommy is mommy," Mika said.

"What about ya triflin ass mother?" Popop said.

And whatever Popop said, Joey wanted to do and be the opposite. He was not to be believed because he was a bad guy. So if that man didn't trust Keisha—if he hated her—Joey would struggle to love her, out of spite if nothing else. But in his strongest memories she always reminded him of winter, even when she managed to hold him tight. *Spoiling that boy*, the men would say. But she birthed that stank boy who needed to get in the shower. This meant something, though Joey could not understand what that something was. He needed the shower so that other kids would stop saying he stank, and maybe he needed the beatings, too, to understand all the things that neither of them could articulate. The boy needed someone to lead him toward something, no matter what that something was. There were just too many unknown unknowns and it was driving him crazy: *How do you add and subtract? And for what? What is deodorant? And toothpaste? Why the stupid teachers think I have time to read the stupid books? Why everybody wanna know about my winkey or doin it or not and with who and how and when and at what time of day? And why they care about God and don't care about no people? And where is God?*

Tia was someone who seemed to have all those answers and more.

"Ya mom a crackhead, boy," she said flatly. "You aint know that? Stop actin retarded. You aint slow." She laughed.

That she was so matter-of-fact made Joey feel a little stupid, but also made him want to follow her more. That Tia agreed with Popop on this matter was a problem, but it was obvious to Joey that Tia was the smartest one around. And sometimes she would even defend him. Whenever Keisha demanded retribution because Joey was trying to hug her while she was high or because he asked the wrong question or cried too much, he would walk into the bathroom as ordered. There, he'd stand naked with a frown, looking away from his own body. Often, Keisha forgot she'd sent him in there, and Joey stayed for hours, thinking about Tia and what he could do to make her like him, how he might become more like her. There were proud moments where Tia would say to Keisha, *Oh, just leave that damn boy alone. You know he just a sissy.* And Keisha would listen. Even if they argued first, adults took Tia seriously. Other times Keisha might waltz into the middle of Joey's thoughts with a black belt that had little metal divots on it and hit him on his back and butt. It hurt, but it was so slow and confusing. She said confusing things between each strike, like *Imma show you,* and *This what you get for playin with me so much,* even when no one had been playing at all.

Joey and Keisha did play, though, and Mika, too. When Keisha was in a good mood, they watched music videos on MTV and the Box, blasting Lauryn Hill and Erykah Badu and 112 and TLC and Aaliyah and Brian McKnight on the big living room TV that Popop found and fixed from the scrap yard across the street. The music was so loud that Joey couldn't think and didn't need to. *These are the times,* Dru Hill sang; and Joey never wanted them to end. The singing and blaring music protected him from his own thoughts, like some kind of myelin sheath around his little neurons. Hearing people sing about love and sadness and loss were a verification. Proof that he wasn't crazy. One day he would make something that did this for other people, that made them feel less invisible or lit on fire by people who kept repeating the force of love.

Erykah Badu's voice soothed Joey into comfort. It untensed his muscles just to hear "Didn't Cha Know" opening, the smooth and beautiful skin of Badu's face spread across sixty inches of television, never ending. He'd run his hand across the screen trying to touch her. *Tried to run but I lost my way,* she sang. Brian McKnight was always starting back at one, so how hard could it be? *Say farewell to the dark night*, he sang, *I see the coming of the sun.* In these moments Joey really did feel like a little child, like life had just begun. TLC was his favorite, though. He would not go chasing any waterfalls, and he certainly could not keep listening to the rivers and the lakes he was used to. The music washed grime off his skin; lonely mud sank into the carpet. He was with other people. These people were his people on television and dancing in the living room. Mika was the cutest little sister in the world then, two inches from the screen, offbeat and with little balance. It took a while for her to round out consonants too, but she was all about a W. She said "Peaches and Cweam" and "Onwy You" or "Wock the Boat" and "Ewything Is Ewything," and Keisha and Joey would not stop laughing.

They asked her to say what her favorite songs were, and with a confidence Joey could not understand Mika blurted them out on command.

"No Scwubs!" Mika said.

Keisha and Joey hit the floor rolling, holding their guts and asking Mika to repeat it over and over again.

"No Scwubs!" Mika said, with more verve than before.

Joey enjoyed this song, too, especially the video, and Keisha knew it.

"Damn, boy, you can't look away from that screen," she said. "You gone be alright?"

And she was smiling when she said this. A rare smile, giggling at the boy's ogling. Joey's obsession with the women on the screen was an affirmation for Keisha. In his staring, she knew she'd done something right. What Joey would have given to be in the same room with Chilli back then: an arm, a leg? His whole damn body? Joey thought about her every day, circling through the outfits from the "No Scrubs" video, about how he would definitely not be a scrub, no matter what. Being a scrub was already out of the question if it meant that Chilli would never love him.

"She not even the cutest one," Keisha said, laughing. "She too skinny." She liked T-Boz the most, though it would take great time and distance before Keisha came home with an appropriately thick girlfriend of her own as an example.

Mika smiled and giggled at everything, her cheeks chunky and round and dimpled and brown. Tia used to walk in on the three of them dancing and singing. She was too cool to participate but she always laughed with them. She chopped Mika and Joey up for thinking that 112 was talking about actual peaches, like the fruit.

"Boy youn't know nothin about eatin no pussy," she said.

Sometimes Popop walked in on the music-blaring, karaoke-singing trio after work. Hearing Joey's lungs crackle through the end of "No Scrubs," the man grimaced and shook his head in disgust.

"See. Yall helpin make that boy a faggot," he said. "Encouragin that shit."

He was loaded up with bags as usual: lunch from work, assorted huggie juices, action figures, chalk and crayons and too-hard candy.

Keisha would suck her teeth. The power of her tooth

sucking was legend, like a million dry-mouthed titans, disappointed with their lot in the world, the thunder of a hundred heavy tongues clacking in unison. "Earl," she said. "You better leave my damn baby alone. Go head somewhere. You always grouchin around and shit all miserable. Go be miserable in ya damn room." She flagged him away, the big muscle in her neck bulging out every time she moved, making it clear that she was getting skinnier than Chilli, who she said was too skinny.

Popop would walk off mumbling curses. He'd drop the bags on the kitchen table and go into his room, snatching up the air in his last word before closing his door. "Ya baby, huh. Lazy ass need to come take care of ya babies. Only come around here to smoke crack when it's too cold to run the streets and eat up all my damn food. Fuckin tired of this shit. You and ya fuckin mother," he said.

Keisha kept dancing. "Oh hush, Earl, I'm workin on it," she said. "Imma get my shit together. You just watch." She said *you just watch* a lot. Then, she turned to Joey in a much lower voice and said, "He the one spoiling yall anyway and rottin ya teeth with all that damn candy and stupid toys."

The next day, she'd be gone. When he was younger, Joey would try to look for her during the day, but eventually, he learned. Before anyone was awake, or just Popop heading to work, he'd watch music videos alone. Incubus's "Drive" was a standout then. Brandon Boyd created himself right in front of Joey's eyes, like an anime character. First person, third person,

2-D, 3-D, it didn't matter. A whole embodied world bristled to life; the boy missed his pencils then; he realized he was missing more but couldn't quite tell what. Boyd was so skinny, like Joey but a white boy with big black earrings and bright red tattoos: a koi fish even, swimming up his arm all strange and exotic. *What a cool weirdo*, Joey thought. *Make Yourself* was not an album but a plan, an imagination heist through a constantly demeaning reality. *Why not try and make yourself?* Boyd sang. *Why not?* Joey thought. Joey imagined his mother kissing him on the cheek the night before, and loving her. Repulsed by morning, he rubbed her off his face.

Joey kept drawing pictures but never quite of himself. That was easy, and all it took was a pencil and paper. Large bodies of water that took up most of the page, and no land in sight, still in the back of the Death Note. A tiny boat with a man inside, possibly a fisherman, or an explorer. The water, translucent. Even though he'd never seen clear, open water like that he knew it existed from movies and the Discovery Channel. In the body of water there were serpents, large ones dwarfing the boat with two, sometimes three, rows of serrated teeth and tongues that forked in three directions. They were getting meaner. They lurked, jaws propped open wide and waiting for a meal beneath the water, ready to swallow the tiny boats and fisherman whole. Sometimes they would show themselves first, just to startle the man in the boat, especially the talking, thinking ones. Joey drew them thinking, *Will I get splinters in my mouth from this boat?* When he learned the word "capsize" from *The Legend of Dragoon* on PlayStation, he went back and changed that to *Will I get splinters from capsizing and then eating this boat?* to make this sea creature sound more intelligent than his peers. One sea creature with six eyes said, *Will this man's raincoat leave a plastic aftertaste?* Practical concerns. The man was always wearing a raincoat, because it always rained. It was always wet and cold. Fish splashed.

Sometimes the sea serpent would ask the man what he was doing there, or why he was eating all the fish, to which the man would not reply and be eaten. Joey figured that the man would be eaten whether he replied or not, so better to keep his dignity. He'd draw hundreds of pages with the serpent and the man in the boat moving, inch by inch, barely perceptible from scroll to scroll, but fluid when flipping through all the pages together in rapid succession. Then he'd color them with colored pencils or stolen oil pastels from Kmart. He was proud of these works of art, but still kind of lonely, so he showed them to his family.

Popop said, "What the fuck is that dumb shit?"

Keisha said they were cute but she was busy.

But they weren't supposed to be cute, they were supposed to be vicious, and at least as serious as the Loch Ness Monster. He worked on making them more vicious. He was drawing and selling them for a dollar a page to old women who walked by the apartment. They didn't comment on the drawings, or the increasingly aggressive dialogue from man to serpent, serpent to man; they just smiled and handed him the dollar with growing looks of concern, confusion on their faces.

As business grew, Joey rotated the drawings to landscapes.

Lengthwise, he couldn't make the water as deep, but the size of the serpent, just a fraction of its body on the page, head rearing up over the boat, implied unknown oceanic depths. It also allowed him to create the tiny islands with those single palm trees. Coconuts grew there, or some hardy, imaginary fruit that tasted better than coconuts, more like frozen Reese's cups. In some of the narrative arcs the man would survive and live happily on the island. He even became friends with the serpent and they exchanged fish for fruit and talked to each other about their problems. The serpent had trouble finding a mate, and so did the man. The serpent told the man about the ocean, and all its creatures and beauty and how there were so few of his kind. The man told the serpent that even though there were too many humans, he was still very lonely.

Joey had never heard of Moby Dick or Herman Melville or any writer for that matter. But he knew that people— not people like him or his family, but people with money and what was often described on commercials as a "sense of adventure"—sometimes paid to be that man on the boat in the raincoat. It was called whale watching. The whole enterprise was terrifying, yet Joey wanted to be a part of it too; perhaps whale watching should be an option, if only to turn it down. He couldn't even swim, but he could certainly fathom what lived in the ocean and decided it should stay on-screen and far away from his own body despite his growing desires for proximity. On television, people cheered when blue whales jumped out of the water just a few feet away from them, splashing everyone on the boat. Did they think the whale cared about them? That it was being careful not to rock the boat, to flip it over? And what about Free Willy? He was smaller, but Joey used to look at all his sharp little teeth and that fake, coy, carnivore smile and wonder how that little boy felt safe sliding his face along the orca's cheek. In the famous scene where Willy jumps out over the boy, Joey could only think of what would happen if Willy fell short. What if Willy miscalculated and landed flat on the little white boy whose arm stretched out for Willy's underside? He'd be crushed. Nothing but a pile of open fractures, flattened by twelve thousand pounds of whale.

And Willy most certainly would not mourn the boy, but find a new pod, a new god, maybe even a less restrictive movie contract. When Joey got caught stealing the oil pastels from Kmart, he asked Popop for the money to buy more. He told Joey that he should stop wasting his time on dumb shit like that and get a fucking job instead of asking him all the time. Then he gave the boy ten dollars. Joey wasn't sure if he wanted to be the man in the raincoat or the serpent. He didn't know who was better off, or if it even mattered. He didn't know what Goku or Yagami Light would do under any of these circumstances, but he knew that he missed having a pet, something furry he could love and hold and touch.

At night Joey would argue with his sister. He considered her an optimist; her fantasies were not dark and therefore not true, just fantasies. The way she thought would only get her hurt. Mika waited for Keisha to return anew, always patient, somewhere between unconditional and delusional in her love. In the darkness Mika would reach out for her brother from one bunk to another, her loneliness palpable. And she'd keep reaching her whole life.

"Joey, I can't wait till Mommy come back to get us," Mika said. "I can't wait."

"Mika, just shut up," Joey said.

"Mommy gonna take us to live with her soon," Mika went on.

"Okay, Mika."

"You not excited?"

"Mika. Just be quiet. For real."

"Mommy is gonna come with her new—"

"Mika, just shut the fuck up right now," Joey whispered, yelled, and cried at the same time. "You so fuckin stupid. Aint nobody comin back here to get nobody, dummy. You gettin on my nerves bein so fuckin stupid. You aint no baby no more," he said. Then he paused for a second, just long enough for his sister to start crying. "Grow up! Grow the fuck up! If we get outta here, it aint gone have nothin to do wit any of them!"

Mika cried, deep and slow. She was so little. Sometimes she covered her head with the pillow because she was scared of both the roaches crawling on her and Joey yelling at her to be quiet. On the nights when he cursed out his little sister, he couldn't sleep either. Guilt and imaginings kept him up. Their mother, like a specter, sometimes crept into the bedroom at night when he thought she was gone, nudging at her first-born to wake up and do something. They were coming to get her. *Help!* she'd say. *Who are they?* the boy would ask. Her eyes widened in anger. *Stop asking dumb questions and help me!* she'd say. *Help!* Joey's sweat ran cold on the top bunk between two worlds.

"Mom, what's wrong! Just tell me!" he said. "What am I supposed to do?" He was crying.

"You gonna let em get me?" she said, inches away from his face, whispering then. Her eyes were terrifying, big and white and bulbous and red. "You just gonna fuckin let em get me, Joey," she said, twisting her neck, then leaning it to one side and leaving it there like she was possessed.

Joey woke up again. She was gone; he'd let them get her. A terrible son. He cursed his little sister instead of protecting her. He ignored his grandmother. What could he be good for? Oldest child, man of the house.

Keisha had told Joey that her water broke in Holmesburg prison. She was visiting Popop, who Joey imagined was being experimented on even though he would never talk about it. Upon discovering this, Joey decided to think he was like Guts in the anime *Berserk*, tossed down out of a corpse womb into a steaming battlefield scrawling with hot demon innards. All he had to do was fight his way out. Giant black claymore in hand, he'd fall in love with a short-haired black girl named Casca who would, inevitably, be raped and killed by his best friend who also, rather than go on living in this world, had decided to become an archdemon. The ex-friend turned archdemon would also eat Joey's left arm for good measure, leaving the boy lonelier and more broken than when he began. It was written. Somewhere it was happening, had happened, and would happen again. In truth, though, Joey was only dropped down the steps once as a baby and nothing magical resulted from the incident. He was born at Episcopal hospital. Pedestrian. Plenty of crack babies to go around because since time immemorial people who did not look like Joey or his mother had ensured that this would be so.

This was also why, Joey supposed, Keisha had to be visiting the prison so often while she was pregnant in the first place. She smuggled in bags of weed in her coochie so Popop could sell them, and it was from this origin story that Joey learned to like the word "coochie," how it felt coming off his lips. Once they got past security, Keisha would slip the baggies to Ganny in the bathroom, who put the baggies in her cheeks like a chipmunk. She gave the baggies to Popop by kissing him, but the strangest part about this story for Joey, even then, was that there was kissing in jail. They all laughed and laughed about the whole plot, but Joey was fixated on the kissing. It was so confusing to think about the fact that someone could come into a jail and kiss someone else, like a cruel amusement for everyone that there were these little pieces of intimacy scattered all around even if you were on permanent state punishment, which had already been determined since before you were born. And not just any kissing. It was kissing between Popop and Ganny. On the mouth, like lovers. Joey just could not picture it. Keisha laughed and laughed at her son's confusion, the jail, the kissing. She laughed and laughed. But she never fully talked to him about giving birth.

It would be difficult to find out later what really happened. She might have been afraid of staying in the hospital, so paranoid and so tired, sick of defending herself from physical and psychological assaults, so she left her baby boy lying in the NICU with the other desiccated little creatures. All Joey knew, really, was that the birth certificate said "Baby Boy," and he guessed she had left. He knew. The discovery would come as a surprise when trying to get a job, and in Baby Boy Joey's attempts to apply to college and join the army. He underestimated it. Just how difficult the whole thing would turn out to be, the forging of an identity without a single person standing by you, testifying on your behalf. Just a piece of paper that said "Baby Boy," like Tyrese in a classic negro B movie.

"I'm sorry, Joey" was what Keisha would say when thick and sober. But she never smiled for real when she was like that. She was both more full and more dead without the drugs; they were a part of her, and always would be. "This is just who I am. I don't wanna stop," she said.

"It's okay, Mom," Joey told her. "Don't worry about that" was what he'd later say in group therapy, or driving her to the parole officer, or in court, or the rehabs.

"Fuck you, and if you died today, it would be too late!" was what he would soon yell at her in middle school.

It seemed that Keisha always knew about Joey and Tia, but she couldn't talk about it without crying. Why? Once, Tia and Joey were sitting on the living room couch with a blanket over them watching *Candyman* or HBO After Dark when Keisha walked into the room acting weird.

Tia shook her head. "Ya mom doin crack again? God damn, how she got time for anything else? That bitch in the bathroom like five times a day." This infuriated Tia and her tiny bladder, having to bang on the door and yell for Keisha to get out. She spoke to Keisha like they were equals. More than technical sisters. *How does Tia know everything?* Joey thought. *Who taught her? Who will teach me?*

Tia and Joey began making a game of Keisha's drug abuse. So much quicker than Mika to give up on his mother's promises, Joey didn't mind toying with the inevitable, the foreverly destitute. And he wanted to impress Tia, always, whether he admitted it or not. He was willing to grasp any chance at short-term pleasure, at any expense. But it didn't begin as a game. He first tried to ignore Keisha. When she came out of the bathroom he would just sigh and go into another room. He would try to play *Digimon.* Joey dragged his little Agumon around the digital world, feeding him and cleaning up his poop and launching fireballs at the other Digimon who'd gone astray. Keisha followed him and asked things like, "Do you see them, Joey?" or "Are you gonna help me?" Seeing his mother's face like that, reflected in the television screen on top of Agumon's hunger-pang squeals, made the boy feel sick. He wondered if Keisha could see the monsters from the digital realm, and how much cooler that would be than the more likely explanation.

It made Tia laugh every time. "Ya mom always fuckin trippin," she said. "She gotta know she look stupid as shit."

Eventually, when Keisha tapped Joey on the shoulder to get his attention, he'd ask her in a forced state of calm, "Please, leave me the fuck alone forever. Please."

But he never wrote her name next to Popop's in the book, just like he never wrote Ganny's. Doing that might make him too much like Popop. The boy figured it was the men who needed to die and the women who could maybe be repaired and redeemed; no telling where he might have picked that up. So he held off. He kept his hatred silent as the book filled with the names of every person at his school, the neighborhood boys like Kevin and Ray, his uncle of the same name who always knocked him to the ground playfully, as if all other interaction was out of the question.

"Get up, Scooter," his uncle would say. "Don't be a little pussy all the time," the man's veins bulging out from every inch of his arms.

Joey wrote his uncle Alley Cat's name, too, for being big and grown and meek, lacking all the gumption he thought an adult man of his size should have, for making no rebuttals to Popop or his brothers for either subtle or blatant damages. And Joey was bewildered with Keisha's claims to love them all. So he and Tia mocked her. They repeated her stutters, saying *uh uh, uh uh* right after her and laughing at her confusion, her twisted facial expressions. While Keisha ignored most talk while she was high, she was acutely responsive to the children's repetitions. They yelled at her to stop being a crackhead. Joey told her it would be much better if she was in jail again; at least there, and for a few days after, she'd be fat and healthy and sober. He told her that it hurt when she acted this way. And he cried so much, as crybabies do, the minute Tia wasn't around. After wiping his tears he told Keisha that she should die. He wanted her to leave and never come back. She'd hit him with something plastic; he'd cry and start over again.

Eventually, in response to Tia's and Joey's most spirited ridicule, Keisha would grab a broom and start smacking them with it. They ran. It was plastic, but they ran anyway. First upstairs and then out to the roof, on top of the Glenloch Street garage. They stayed there until Keisha got tired and sobered up, but she was still big mad, scowling at them from the bedroom window, afraid to step out.

"Y'all gotta come down eventually. Shit. Think I'm fuckin playin," she said.

While they waited, Joey tried to kiss Tia and she frowned and pushed his head away.

"What you doin?" she said.

He didn't know how to respond. They sat on the roof quietly, waiting for his mother to cool down. He thought of jumping from the roof and running off, but to where? With what? Keisha stayed angry after that for a long time, but they could tell she felt silly about the whole thing.

These constant happenings only increased Joey's determination to break his sister's optimism where their mother was concerned. He wanted to prove that he was right before Keisha could do it herself.

"Why you believe everything she say?" Joey said, exasperated from the start.

"Because it's Mommy," Mika said.

"You so fuckin stupid," Joey said. "God I can't stand you. Good night."

But he still had the urge to talk, not just because he was lonely, but because even when it wasn't his mother, he always felt something large and paranormal looming in the darkness. Perhaps as the most persistently simple subconscious threat, he thought there must be aliens watching him. The random lights flashing by outside not to be confused for cars. Even Courage the Cowardly Dog knew. Those silicon aliens from true abduction stories, humanoid with big gray oval heads and black eyes, were waiting. Every night one of them stood next to his bed, ready to snatch him away if he dared to look at them. If he stayed quiet long enough, and kept his eyes closed, he might make it through the night. Whether or not he slept was irrelevant. An alien might take him somewhere and have its way with him; it would touch him in ways that he did not want. Anytime he was not communicating, not talking with his sister, he could see the alien in the darkness, and no amount of blinking would dull its gray skin, would shut out the long fingers reaching into his skull through his ears, nose, eyes, and mouth. Whenever a roach fell from the ceiling with a little plop onto the bedspread or railing he jumped up, shrieking. He knew they were coming to get him. Mika laughed at his screeching but pretended she wasn't, to spare him maybe.

"Shut up," Joey would say. "Shut the fuck up."

Mika giggled herself to sleep.

Joey lay up all night thinking. Maybe he would prefer his mother to the aliens.

In Joey's earliest Halloween memories, he was a toilet paper mummy. He wanted more than anything to be scary, to intimidate other bodies beyond a reasonable doubt, and his mother—whose expertise in terror relied on the fact that she was on parole at the time—had little on offer outside the dry-as-dust two-ply tissue paper desiccated on the bathroom floor. He stood in front of the mirror, spinning around on his toes while she held the roll, draping his body in tissue. There was little doubt that he was the only toilet tissue mummy in Frankford. But the toilet paper mostly slid off his narrow shoulders and flew away in the wind; sometimes the chalky taste of it got caught in his mouth and turned sopping wet before dissolving. It was half-ply toilet paper, he thought then, the kind of stuff that, even after looping it three or four times around one hand, would somehow return damp after vigorous wiping. If one was too rough, say, his mother's stiff fingers on one mummified clavicle, it would shred. Other kids noticed that, not only was he a "shitty tissue mummy," which was a "corny ass, bitch nigga costume" in the first place, but they soon deduced that he was also poor, a fact that all the socially apt kids were wise enough to conceal by now behind off-brand Timberlands and huge cubic zirconia earrings, in the left ear only for boys, of course, signifying their unquestionable straightness.

He blamed his mother for the failure. They sat on the couch just a foot away from each other, him crying, her eyes bulging from their sockets and reminding him over and again that they were coming to get her. What would Joey do about it? Afterward, she pretended it never happened. Then she was gone. But, in spite of a broadening disillusionment with the world, Joey continued to invest in Halloween as best he could. The boy took costume matters into his own hands. Jack Skellington, it seemed to him, was the next obvious choice; he was lanky and goofy, too, both grotesque and joyful together. They might be unified, singing happy songs through the night. *This is Halloween! This is Halloween!* Plus, everybody loved Jack. Those costumes, though, were expensive, and he'd already been banned from Kmart for stealing Gundam Wing model kits and one sexy, muscular Spider-Man action figure whose unusually articulate joints could be guided into eighteen different battle positions. If Joey was going to be something that was neither himself nor Jack Skellington, it had to be a more practical kind of terrifying.

Vampirism was always right under the boy's nose, beckoning. Lusting. He stole plastic fangs from magic shops, and capes were just pieces of any black shirt or sheet recombined with scissors. Makeup was always around. Fangs had the added bonus of covering his own teeth, those things he'd practiced hiding day in, day out like his mouth might break something open that hurts to close. Always on his mind was that big black cavity up front and the gap that seemed to be widening as the Bugs Bunnies pushed out parallel to the ground. He strained his tongue, trying to push his own inborn incisors flat and normal. At home, he was Mr. Ed, but they were more creative at school. There was only one kid whose teeth were worse than his, but that kid could fight, as he demonstrated on Joey during the first week of class. So Joey was a vampire, always. He'd been obsessed with vampires for a while before officially turning to the dark side. Eternal life meant possibilities, starting over, changing things, having a better family, more friends maybe. All the best characters, the ones he thought he could trust, were vampires: Alucard, Raziel, Vincent, Saya, Abel, Lestat, and even Timmy Valentine. The last few especially. *Vampire Junction* was the only book the boy would ever read. He'd find it in the basement. Popop would catch him several times but fail to stomp it out of Joey's mind completely.

"Always doin some little sissy white boy shit," the man would say, forcing Joey to stow away the text. "Need to get off ya ass and do some fuckin work around here."

Technically, Joey wasn't on his ass thumbing through the yellowed pages; he was standing, but decided, for once, to keep the articulation of this overlooked technicality to himself. And work often meant the sink and the outside, the grime in all directions never satiated or exhausting itself. That sink lay always clogged, mismatched dishes stacked high and exasperating, the orange slime of days-gone ravioli bound inside of blue bowls like the residue of an older but no less vile civilization. Work meant grabbing the trash in the summer with all the maggots dripping wet and rotting through plastic or holes poked open by long-dead blue crabs, their shells desperate breeding grounds for *Musca domestica* which, upon his discovering the scientific name for those diabolical creatures who'd spread cholera and typhoid to Joey's entire simulated community in a long-lost PC game, felt more fitting than the all-too-gentle nomenclature "housefly." One time, Joey slung a heavier bag over his shoulder and found little clusters of maggots squished up against his ankles, right under the socks after he came in to shower; he freaked out, flushing the socks down the toilet, clogging that, too. Confusion was absolute. What the suggested work-over-books balance told Joey was that physical prowess mattered and everything else was for white people, who were apparently meek. Life, then, was first and foremost a war for survival, a kind of social Darwinism shrouded by a veneer of toughness and the imprisonment of only speaking when spoken to. In this schema, the subtext was that physically helpless white people couldn't survive, or perhaps just didn't need to be as strong. Fitting, then, that Joey's closest friend was the little white boy who lived upstairs and in and out of *Star Ocean*.

The most comforting part of their friendship was that their mothers smoked crack together, though they rarely mentioned it directly, perhaps because there was no need; everybody either was somebody or knew somebody or loved somebody who was doing crack back then; it was the weather. And Jeremy and Joey were like brothers under the storm for a bit, both too quiet and gentle for their surroundings and lacking all avenues out of this shared softness. Beneath the surface, though, there was always a slight disconnect between him and Jeremy that they both refused to name, perhaps out of fear that it would break the only tie they had.

Without naming it, sometimes frustration boiled up between them and might manifest through seemingly unrelated disagreements. It was petty at its finest. They would decide to dislike something that the other person adored without citing any real evidence or reasoning; so Joey hated *Star Wars* and Jeremy despised vampires. In fact, "fuck *Star Wars*" became, for a time, Joey's favorite phrase. But, had he had the language then, Joey might have surmised that Jeremy simply didn't need vampires the way he did.

Despite how white their worlds were, Joey was obsessed with Timmy Valentine and Lestat, not just because of the power they held as night stalkers, but because they harbored such intense intellectual passions; they were completely unlike anyone he deserved to know. They hurt people, but not for hurting's sake. They inhaled music and art, breathing it back out like CO_2 for anyone bold enough to come near them. They were not just an escape for him, but an infinite expression of possibility. He resented the lack of seriousness given to his attempts at writing and drawing comics. He never knew anyone who considered college, or was just happy with their adult life, and that pissed him off in ways that he couldn't explain at the time. He was jealous of Timmy and Lestat, who got to convene with people that cared about thinking and art and learning for its own sake, as sparse as those people may have been. Both vampires were also renowned musicians. When Joey was sad, he imagined himself playing and singing "Scar Tissue," but he didn't have a guitar or sheet music or motivation. There wasn't even a person he could safely describe a fantasy like that to.

While forced to finish *Vampire Junction* in private, Joey got to be a fucking hero out in the open with his vampire costumes on Halloween. Just the thought of immortality, super strength, and shape-shifting boosted his confidence. Anime music videos of Alucard and Seras massacring armies of fake vampires and lapping up their blood played on repeat in Joey's head. Alucard smiled and transformed into a pack of black dogs, slurping up the gooey bits of bad guys with his extra-long tongue. Seras waded through bullets, her eyes beet red, exploding heads with a grenade launcher, razor-sharp teeth shredding the bodies of ill-prepared men. There would be no foul play while Joey roamed the street in his fangs and cape. The other good thing about vampire costumes was how adaptable they were, "adaptable" being another one of Joey's favorite words, like the adapter to hook up the game to the TV was different from the way he was failing to adapt to his environment at home and at school but not as a vampire. As he got older, and much larger, it didn't seem ridiculous to just throw on some fangs and go trick-or-treating. Sure, the fangs from the year before might smell bad, but he could always soak them like dentures first. There was also a magic shop right around the corner on Frankford Ave that sold fangs cheap when the stealing got too obvious, his bigger, clumsier body giving him away. They had these little plastic frogs and lizards too, that Joey could place in a bowl of water to let grow overnight, which for a while he used as proof of his magical abilities. Still, other kids caught on to it eventually, and he quit the cape and makeup and magic and ended up with just fangs. A more refined vampire, hiding in plain sight, passing. He never really let go of that feeling of invincibility, though, the fantasy that in some way he might make it all real.

He walked the streets alone at night just praying that some vampire would choose him. Some night stalker would swoop down from a rooftop, a bat would transform right in front of him; maybe the fog on a dreary day would take human shape. And not just any human. Most of them looked like this tall Puerto Rican girl from school named Crystal, or Erica, who'd moved away, to college maybe, after he'd caught her playing Catch a Girl Freak a Girl but failed to do it with her properly under the ramp where they sold soft pretzels at Stearne Elementary. They'd suck the blood and cells and molecules out of Joey's neck, his hands, his hips, his thighs. They'd wrap his limp body in warmth and red like Vincent did Cloud and spirit the boy through an open window in which a canopy bed with silk sheets lay in the middle of a room catching every drop of moonlight. Things would happen in that bed; Joey didn't know exactly what, but they would happen, and they would feel very, very good. The boy even practiced the lines, saying yes over and over, begging to be turned, so he wouldn't come off too eager and suspicious. His mother caught him moaning in bed half-soaked once, begging Aaliyah to kill him after watching *Queen of the Damned*. "*Please*," he said, pressed up against the twin mattress, his hips avoiding the springs, "*Please*, Queen Akasha." Nothing could have convinced him that vampirism wasn't the most superior mode of existence, though Jeremy tried to make the case that Super Saiyans or Jedi or some shit were better.

While Joey went on thinking he was cool in costume, he came to realize that few other people were taking him seriously outside of Jeremy, and the pair started trick-or-treating on their own. Joey's mother was in jail again by then, and Popop wouldn't take them. It was past time for them to grow up anyway, become men. Jeremy's dad wasn't around much anymore, either, and his mom had his baby brother to deal with. Both boys felt kind of old to be escorted anyway, to have their hands held for anything, even if it was what they really needed. All the other kids were trick-or-treating alone, so they would too. Not only was it a chance to earn some desperately needed street credit by showing their independence, but they could cover more ground without old people holding them back, which meant more candy. Joey's memory of what Jeremy was that year is vague, but he could remember that it was neither cool nor scary enough, so likely a Jedi.

They made a killing on candy, targeting Mayfair mostly. It was better than their own neighborhood in every way; the farther northeast you went from Frankford, the better off you were. Homeowners had better treats. There were lots of lawns, several parks with large fields that didn't have glass in them, and basketball courts with nets. The people in Mayfair liked to decorate their houses both inside and out for holidays. They'd have pumpkins on porches and ornaments hanging from the trees in their front yards. There were fake witches and skeletons everywhere laughing maniacally and jangling in the wind. Old white ladies came to the doors smiling with buckets full of king-sized Snickers bars and Milky Ways, Reese's Cups and Skittles, big bags of Herr's potato chips, sour straws and Twizzlers, and best of all, money. Yes, some of these old ladies put money in their doubled-up Save-A-Lot trick-or-treat bags, especially if they ran out of candy, so sometimes it was smart to double back. There were dollars here and there, on rare occasions a five or some two-dollar bills, but it was money. It was heaven or Halloween Town or something better left lingering unnamed in the moment.

He and Jeremy were proud of that first year alone. By the time they finished, their bags were so heavy that they had to stop to catch their breath several times on the walk home. Not a block out of Mayfair, though, they saw some older kids who clearly weren't trick-or-treating, walking toward them on the same side of the street. They both knew what to do and silently crossed to the other side, hoping to turn down a different block, but the detour was too late, too conspicuous. They had already been spotted. Both boys tried to keep walking normally, deep in denial. While appearing unafraid never really helped, it was better than nothing. But the other boys had already made their decision, probably long before they'd even seen Jeremy and Joey. They sped up. And when they came within arm's reach of both the younger boys, Jeremy and Joey were still trying to act casual. One of the older kids jumped in front of them, blocking their path.

"Fuck is this, young boul?" he said, sliding his hand under Joey's trick-or-treat bag slow, feeling the heft of it. He was wearing a skully and smelled like cigarettes, probably from his unkempt beard. Joey guessed that he and his friend were from Frankford High or Northeast.

The other two boys behind them started laughing. "Leave that little faggot alone," one of them said. "Nigga might piss on hisself."

Joey was almost certain he'd never seen the boys before despite how familiar their bodies felt next to his, like a reflection of the only older boys he'd ever know, those destined to become the only men he knew, whose bodies were just like his and his like theirs, all of them terrified to admit this to themselves or each other. Joey and Jeremy both kept quiet and still, hoping they would just get bored and go away. Speed-walking in the opposite direction would have made the fear too obvious, and turning their backs to the older boys at this point was out of the question. Jeremy's eyes turned to Joey as if he was going to do something, like he should do something.

It always felt like Jeremy expected certain things of Joey, because he was black like everyone else they knew and bigger. But both their frames were like stick bugs, as per the neighborhood rumors that they might both blow away in a high wind. And still, Joey felt that Jeremy thought Joey should be able to fight for real. Whenever they'd wrestle, Joey won. He was always stronger. So when they talked about getting picked on in school, Jeremy seemed to resent his friend for not fighting back, for not defending either of them. He couldn't understand why Joey wasn't just laying waste to bullies instead of crying about it. In this, Joey came to think that Jeremy had the same oversimplified Man Up approach in common with Popop. In their WWF days, Jeremy would turn red and grow furious at Joey for hurting him sometimes and then laughing, which only made it worse. But that was just play. There were no moral implications and Joey never felt bad about winning or losing, even when Jeremy's older brother Daniel would whoop both their asses. Joey struggled with how to tell Jeremy, or anyone else, that even though he was so tall, taller than two of the high school kids stopping them now, he just didn't have the confidence to defend himself physically. He didn't want to; he didn't want to have to punch someone in the face because he didn't like how it felt.

Now the boys were chuckling and making jokes among themselves while both Jeremy and Joey stood still. The boy in front of them reached into Jeremy's bag and grabbed a handful of candy, then he threw it all on the sidewalk. It rattled on the concrete. "Fuck you gone do, white boy?" he said.

At first, Joey assumed Jeremy would swing on him. He'd been kicked out of schools for fighting even though he never started it. No one believed that, of course. They just kept shuffling him along to rougher schools, amplifying his anger. Joey was afraid to follow that example. Eventually Jeremy got sent away for high school. With Jeremy's résumé alone, one would have expected him to whoop all kinds of ass, but he rarely won a fight. He was just brave, and scrappy. When the handful of his candy was grabbed, Jeremy put one foot forward, grounding himself. Then, the kid in front of them grabbed Jeremy's whole bag of candy and started to pull, but Jeremy wouldn't let go. The kids from behind started laughing harder and pointing. One of them strolled in front of the two boys and hit Jeremy on the cheek with a flat-fisted haymaker. The candy bag tore, spilling all the treats onto the street, some of which flew into a sewage drain.

Another boy from behind grabbed Joey's bag and flung it into the sky. As that plastic bag snapped the candy shot out in different directions as if propelled from the center of an explosion, each piece, the Snickers and Reese's Cups, licorice and gummy bears and Laffy Taffys rapidly taking their own premeasured distances. Later, when teased for being unable to swim, when white kids in college would ask how Joey made it when so many didn't, he would think about the difference between sinking and buoyancy, between flight and failure, as he remembered the candy trickling down around them, having no idea where each piece would fall amid the open secret of prearranged physics, which nevertheless demanded he act on it every second of every single day. Before the last piece even hit the ground, the older boys all ran away, still laughing. Joey and Jeremy were too mad to cry and too proud to pick anything up. The bags were shredded anyway. Joey was just relieved that they were gone. At this point he'd only been beaten up too badly once, and he did not want a repeat from three older boys wearing Timbs. Jeremy's cheek was red, but he wasn't bleeding. He kept mumbling things like "grimey ass dudes…" but he wasn't talking to Joey, at least not directly. They walked home, slow and silent.

Before cable news sought out black people to label thugs, Jeremy's favorite line, "grimey ass dudes" was the closest thing to coded language, Joey felt, for niggers. Even though they shared similar feelings at the time, it hurt to hear him say it. Joey was just as resentful of the black men and boys in their neighborhood, so it was hard to disagree with him. Maybe he should have more often, teetering as he was between believing Jeremy could never harbor racist sentiment and the fact that everyone obviously did; either way, he felt sick. Joey might have referred to those boys as grimey too, but hearing Jeremy say it reminded him to resist the urge whenever he could, reminded him that there was always someone watching and how different it felt, depending on who might be watching and for what reason. It seemed that all it took for Jeremy to refer to someone as a grimey ass dude was for them to be black and in close range, therefore a threat. It was so often preemptive. And Joey was ashamed, so piled up with loathing himself, that he shared those same exact sentiments, out of fear. That was why they didn't need to speak to each other before crossing the street in unison. Joey couldn't outright deny that everyone who ever started such a conflict with them—or Jeremy, for that matter—was undeniably black, like most of the kids in their neighborhood. He just couldn't stand to admit it, or feel like it would never end.

Jeremy never held back mentioning that fact as they got older. Basketball snatched on the court? Black kids. Fights at school? Black kids. Something stolen from him? Black. Kids. Sometimes Joey tried, in vain, to articulate the reasons why things were how they were, but he didn't really have the language, and their material reality was hard to dispute; they could neither travel back in time nor imagine a future that would hurt any less. Joey just wished there was at least one person, one nonfictional character he could point to, that exception to the rule that they might know for real, who might disseminate hope or be nice for the full length of a day. But there wasn't. Silenced by his own childish rage and shame toward other black people, particularly his own family, Joey regularly half agreed with Jeremy, who was all about meritocracy. Black people were clustered in the ghetto because they were lazy, but Jeremy was there, too, which didn't seem to make sense. In Jeremy's mind, there was no racism, and if there was, it was everyone else's discrimination against him. He was indignant about all the grimey black kids targeting him and only him so regularly, and knew, consciously or not, that there was language he could use to denigrate them as a whole. So he did. And he thought if Joey were just tougher, like him, but in a bigger, blacker body, he'd be immune to the terror they both felt every waking day. Over the years of their friendship, that disagreement would eventually drive a wedge between them. As kids, though, and in his currently smacked state, Joey knew a conversation could go nowhere, nor was he calm enough to try and articulate anything at all.

Joey could remember little about the walk home itself, just how he withdrew into his mind while his legs kept moving. He considered, though, that no one would have dared to take Alucord's candy, had he needed it. Some people, who were not actually people, were not to be played with. Had Joey been the kind of creature he'd always dreamed of, who other people demanded he be, he could have ripped those older kids to pieces. Ground their bones into the sidewalk. He wanted them to beg for their lives while he strangled them one by one, watching their fluids drip out into those wedges unifying the concrete. But he couldn't, and he knew, some-how, that he would regret it if he could, reconciling some larger plight when it was all too late. Still, it was hard to deny how the joy of imagining sustained him. And internally, Joey wouldn't stop with just them, either. He'd decapitate everyone in his neighborhood, at his school, in Philly, who acted like them. There would be plenty of bodies. He'd make his mother a vampire so she could kill every boyfriend who beat her down the stairs, then he'd feed them to Jeremy, his reluctant but vampiric sidekick. He'd make Ganny a vampire and she'd murder Popop herself. He'd start a business where kids who were getting pummeled through school for the crime of living could pay him to remove fingernails and drain blood, extract and toss ligaments, burn corneas. And no one would be able to do anything about it.

The cops couldn't just come and arrest everybody standing outside, so maybe his mother wouldn't even be in jail or off wherever she was. She'd have no reason to run, no want for crack, no dependency on men. She'd have no excuse then. If only there was some lab accident or genetic mistake he could exploit, maybe some mutant X gene trials that he might slide into and grant him more than asthma or diabetes or lead poisoning. Something. He welcomed every imaginative solution that might make him feel less weak because he knew there would never be any real ones. But eventually, he became too angry even to imagine. And that, he would later think, was the real loss.

RESIDENT EVIL TOO

No matter how much you board up the windows they just keep coming. And to think, Joey might find reprieve inside a police station. What a strange predicament. Mika yells at him every time she hears an ominous groan. But with so many zombies outside, just walking around Raccoon City like they own the place, it seems a completely rational choice to make, what with it being his first day on the job in the Raccoon City police department and Claire seemingly the only real human who made it, might as well try the coppers.

"Why you lost in the cop station, Joey? Why you lost in the cop station?" Mika keeps saying over his shoulder.

Julian chimes in from his corner, "Powice station! Powice station!"

Joey, now Leon, will help Claire find her brother. He'd never really been inside a police station before, though, and was mostly surprised that it could be so much fun. There were statues and puzzles and deep dark corridors and items lying around everywhere like one big scavenger hunt (who left those bullets on the couch like that?). And there was also this dying black guy named Marvin, too. Marvin knew that Leon was a rookie and so decided to look out for him, tossed him a few items, and ordered Leon to let him die. *As long as you make it out safe.* From Joey's perspective, there was little left of Marvin anyway. Nothing to save.

"Help him, Joey!" Mika yells, tugging on Joey's arm.

"Chill, Mika! You gonna get us all killed," Joey says. He considers turning on the light.

So strange to have an abdominal wound like that. How exactly was Marvin fighting off the attack? Was it Marvin's fault that he got his stomach ate up? Was this victim blaming? Perhaps his selflessness extended further, even before Joey/ Leon the rookie police officer, to some prior moment where a heroic Marvin dove in waist deep to rescue a helpless civilian and got caught up. Would Marvin have helped Mika like Leon wanted to help Claire?

"Joey, he's bleeding!" Mika says.

"Oh my God, Mika, I know. I'm tryna read what they sayin!" he says.

"What they sayin?" Mika asks.

"It's an underground tunnel in here somewhere, Mika. We gotta find it."

And soon as Joey feels safe inside the police station it's Marvin who tells him, in no uncertain terms, that he needs to get the fuck out. But how? *Of course*, he says. *Through the basement.* How in the world did Marvin know where all this started? Do all police departments have basements where they keep the bodies and secret escape routes in case of the ongoing zombie apocalypse? After all, Raccoon City didn't look much different from Frankford or down Erie, not far from where Joey was born, or Kensington and Allegheny some nights where he might, accompanied by Tia, have been riding bikes and gotten purposely lost and called Daddy by his mom's friends. Where someone might offer to suck Joey's winkey or ask Tia what she was doing out there so late and if she wanted to go home with them.

Where was the escape route?

Nevertheless Joey heeds Marvin's words.

"Joey, watch out!" Mika yells, as Joey is licked by a skinless flesh monster. "He lickin you!"

"I know, Mika, I'm tryna get away. Calm down!" he says.

"Lickin," Julian says.

He shoots up the zombies and such and rounds up puzzle pieces so he can roll out Raccoon City. Maybe. But where will he go? He wanted to ask Marvin, before he inevitably died, what else there was outside Raccoon City. Why even bother leaving? Had Marvin ever turned on the television? Despite this turn of events Joey trudges on all through the basement and runs into an alligator. Not nearly as nice as Rex, but what Rex might have been had Joey kept him.

"Oh no, Joey, it's a awagator!" Mika yells.

"Shit! No!" Julian yells.

And Joey wonders for just a second what they did with Rex before destroying this new creature with a grenade launcher, blood and guts splattering all over the sewer.

How much can I buy with my stamps?" Keisha said, flipping through the candy sale catalog.

Joey couldn't tell if she was joking or not, though he definitely wanted her to be joking. He frowned.

"Why you lookin like that? I asked you a question, boy. You tryna sell candy ain't you?" His mother stood with one hand on her hip.

He didn't want to let her down, in case she was being earnest, so it was hard to respond. "Mom, I don't think they allow that," he said. You couldn't even get hot food at the corner store with paper food stamps back then.

"Well, you gotta ask em, then. Did you go ask em?" she said. "Always think you know everything. You don't know everything, Joey. Shit. Get on my fuckin nerves."

Every year before Christmas, Joey's school had a big candy sale where the kids could win prizes. Teachers and principals sent the kids out door-to-door like sweet-toothed perfume ladies or Jehovah's Witnesses. This was probably before, but might have been after Tia and Joey were threatened with a shotgun for playing knock knock zoom zoom. Most kids made big sales from their family's friends and coworkers.

"Mom, I'm pretty sure you can't buy any with those," Joey said again, trying not to sound condescending.

"Whatever, Joey. Fuck you and that candy, then. How the hell you know? You don't know everything, Joey," she said. "Go ask that nigga Earl then."

The boy started to notice a pattern. Whatever he thought should be obvious to everyone would frustrate people if he said it out loud. Sometimes it would get him slapped or beaten. He discovered that mentioning the wetness of water, even if asked, would end in violence. Joey only spoke to Popop on a need-to-know basis. The man did not permit small talk, light talk, or personal talk. But he had money. The old man was reliable for candy sales; Popop had all the money and all the coworkers, meager as they both might have been. Sometimes the guys from Popop's job, including Joey's uncle Walt, would drink at their apartment or crack open blue crabs on the porch. They all knew Keisha's boy. They all knew he suddenly learned to speak up come candy sale time.

Joey walked into Lustrik Corp. with a bunch of brochures, past the cranes and dust, like he owned the place. He'd been there so many times before, even Popop's boss knew him.

"Hey, Joey, you coming to cut the grass again?" the old man said.

"No, not today. But I'm selling candy. You should look at this." He handed the man a brochure. Joey knew all the men at Popop's job who had wives and kids at home and who would spend the most money on bullshit.

"You out here sellin that damn candy?" Popop said, laughing. "Calm down, cutty. I'll just take some in and have people mark down what they want."

Popop took the brochures, and his coworkers bought up the overpriced chocolate-covered cherries, gummy worms, and fancy chocolate hearts and ducks. "It's for Joey, you know, Joey, my peanut-head grandson," Popop told them all. "He gettin all As at school, too, cutty. Help em out. They bout to skip him a grade."

Joey never skipped a grade or went to the "mentally gifted" section either. He was more afraid than smart, but fear, or punkishness, it seemed, was a sign of intelligence, a great relief to overburdened and underprepared teachers who, despite their intentions, were constantly failing themselves and the students anyway. Plus, folks at home refused to sign the paperwork. Popop loved to brag about how smart his grandson was, too smart for his own good. Keisha bragged, too, and Joey couldn't stand it, but this was a lesser battle in a long war of hypocrisy. Joey was rarely interested in the brochure candy itself, except for the chocolate-covered cherries. There was a penny candy store next to Birds, Birds, Birds that sold most everything else. And next to that was a deli with turkey and cheese hoagies that tasted so good Joey could hardly imagine the meat fashioned from some ugly turkey. Knowing the brochures were suspect,

Joey was in it for the prizes. It was the year of the Twister Tyco RC Car and the mad expensive Duncan Yo-yo. The Easy-Bake Oven was done. It was a mobile home for roaches now, and upon closer inspection, Joey realized it was just a low-wattage microwave for kids. Dumb kids who fell for that kind of shit. He was like ten or something and so over it.

He had real problems now. Adult problems. He needed to sell candy to get that Tyco RC Car just as much as he needed to figure out this black thing looming in his mouth. A jagged mass, like dying coral, just appeared in front of his left canine. It both drew attention away from and toward the gap between his teeth. The goal post. Kids at school called it the Black Hole. They would jump away from him whenever he walked by and scream, "Don't let me get sucked in!" And the other kids would come and pull on the kid getting fake-sucked into the tooth. Ten or fifteen of them would form a line like they were playing team tug-of-war. They prepared for battle in the halls, even had spaceship names for the battle against the monster, Shitmouth. This husky white kid coined the name. Joey cried about it as all the other kids circled and pointed in amazement, grabbing his upper lip to peek inside at the dangerous thing.

"Triflin," they said.

"You need ChapStick."

"Rotten," another one followed.

It must have been the girl he liked, Crystal, who said, "It's just a cavity, I don't know why y'all so hype. It's nasty, but still."

After Joey finished crying in the bathroom one day, a teacher pulled him aside and gave him a plastic toothbrush and a little tube of Crest, which kids thought was hilarious. "It's just gonna get sucked into the tooth!" they said. At home, Ganny said it was because Joey ate too much candy. But candy was cheap and made him happy; there had to be other alternatives.

Eventually, when Keisha was home for a bit, she said, "Here boy, you want me to teach you how to brush ya teeth?"

But it was too late. All day and night the boy scrubbed, using whole tubes of toothpaste sometimes and nothing happened. The blackness in the tooth wouldn't go away, and writing down the husky white boy's name wouldn't make him die. Joey grew out his fingernails and tried to pull the tooth out by hand but all he got was plaque. Popop told him to tie a string around it with the other end to the doorknob, then slam the door. All that did was make the boy's gums bleed. It was lodged in there deep. Nothing he could do. Joey tried a kitchen knife, too; he wanted to leverage it out but got nothing but cuts. Every morning he spent hours in the mirror scraping as much of the blackness off as he could with a knife, his fingers, a flathead screwdriver, anything, but it was never enough. It dug in deeper the harder he tried to pull it out. So the boy changed the way his mouth worked. He spoke even less around other people. He refused to smile ever and contorted his jaw muscles in such a way to produce minimal tooth visibility. It changed his voice. Apparently, this made him sound even more gay. Kids would smile and stare at him all class waiting for him to slip up and show the tooth by accident.

At home, Mika was getting bigger and even she said Joey had a dumb, shitty tooth, to which he pushed her and she stumbled on the carpet. Popop slapped him for it, a big hand twisting the boy's head around.

"Don't you go hittin no girl like some lil bitch," he said.

And so the world surrounding the tooth was hopeless. But that Twister Tyco RC Car was not; he could win. He would win.

Joey must have walked the entire Frankford neighborhood peddling candy. He stopped at the homes of both white families knowing they had money and would buy something; he went to the old dudes at the hoagie store under the El; the Asian man at Birds, Birds, Birds; he took the brochure to Fly Guy's barbershop; walked into the local Boys & Girls Club; and he even went to the grocery store and hustled the dude behind the counter where Popop always played his numbers and bought scratch-offs. Popop made good with his coworkers, too. He even bought some himself. All told, Joey had sold over six hundred dollars' worth of candy. It was more money than he'd ever counted to before, and he felt powerful holding on to the thick envelope. With that much money, he could buy new sneakers or new teeth. *But which one would help more?* he thought. Maybe he could buy his own house or a car. He could live off this money. He could do anything with enough money. In the midst of his thinking this, Popop sealed the envelope and whispered to Joey, "You better hide it."

But Joey didn't really know why. And there was only one more day before he had to turn in the envelope to school anyway. He knew that Ganny stole video games sometimes, but she wouldn't steal money that technically wasn't even his. That would be immoral, and Ganny was desperate, not immoral. Besides, if anyone was going to take the money for themselves it would definitely be Joey. He looked up at Popop, confused.

"Don't let ya mom know you got money," he said. "Don't tell that bitch nothin."

It sounded unnecessary; Keisha had never stolen anything from her son. Yes, she got high in front of the kids, sure, but she wasn't a thief. She called her own mother out on stealing all the time, and Ganny called her out on doing drugs in front of the children. Joey saw Keisha as a comparatively reasonable person when sober; it was just difficult for her to stay that way. Popop was just making things up to bolster infighting. It made Joey flustered that Popop thought he knew Keisha better than anyone else. Excited about the sales, though, he couldn't wait to tell his mom that he was gonna get that Twister Tyco RC Car. He ran back into the kitchen to find her, but she was walking out of the bathroom in a cloud of burnt chemicals. In his excitement, he didn't notice the smell soon enough.

"Mom, look at this." He unfolded the brochure to show her.

"Uh-uh. Hmmm. Uh-uh," she grunted. Her right arm was folded across her chest like a dead chicken, her hand clasping her left elbow. Her cheek was nestled in her left palm. With every muttering, her body tensed as if she were receiving mild electrical shocks. Her eyes bulged fierce, mostly white with tiny, dark irises smothered by engorged blood vessels.

"I fucking hate you," Joey said. Then he went to play *Monster Rancher*. He battled his dinosaur creature named Spike in the arena, fed Spike steak and checked on him in the stables, pet the dinosaur to see him nuzzle up against the screen until Joey's eyes sagged. That night he slid the envelope with all the money in it between his mattress and the slats that held it up, managing a secret smile that was just for himself.

The next morning, a Saturday, Joey woke up on the floor. But before going into the living room, he had to make sure he wasn't dreaming last night with all that money, so he reached under the slats for the fat manila envelope. It was gone. His breathing was too shallow. Too quick. Trying to calm himself down, he walked slowly to Popop's bedroom door and knocked only once.

"What you want, Joey?" he said, barely lucid.

"Popop, my candy sale envelope gone!" Conflicting emotions were vying for space in his head: anger, sadness, confusion. More anger. Popop told him to come into the room, which was strange enough in itself. Ganny lay silent and as one with the bed, looking dead.

"Where ya mom at?" Popop said, standing up from the red sheets with his dick hanging out.

Joey hadn't even thought of his mother until Popop brought her up. Every time something went missing, it was Ganny who pawned it. It was Ganny who, every Christmas without fail, would swoop in like the negro Grinch and snatch half the items Popop purchased on drowning credit. Not Keisha.

"I don't know, Popop. She was here last night. I saw her," Joey said.

"Stinkin bitch. Imma kill that bitch, you watch," the man said, his face lingering between a frown and a smile. He sat back on his bed. "Imma kill her." He kept saying it, face in his palms. Popop paused to look up at Joey. "Stop cryin, cutty," he said. "Just stop cryin. You always cryin all the damn time."

Keisha was gone for a long time.

On Monday, Joey got a new envelope and Popop replaced the lost money with his own. The man did this begrudgingly, but not like when Joey asked for five dollars here and there to get cheesesteaks or snacks. It was clearer this time. At least Joey imagined that this was not his fault; he was not being blamed for the missing envelope in the same way he was blamed for being hungry.

And the money wasn't enough. Not for the Twister Tyco RC Car. There was some miscalculation. Something in the math between dollars and sales points that Joey misunderstood; the brochure's language, he learned, was made to be misunderstood. Everything was made to be misunderstood down a long chain of misdirection—another of Joey's favorite words, via the *Monster Rancher* TV show—from people who sat on thrones or in offices, down through Popop and through people like kids and the drug addicted. With over six hundred dollars in sales, Joey had less than two hundred points. Two hundred points was enough for a yo-yo that lit up when you spun it, or a few boxes of candy. Joey scarfed down boxes of gourmet sour worms and one box of chocolate-covered cherries, cooled until frozen in the freezer. He sucked the insides of the chocolate-covered cherries out, spitting the sticky fruit part on the pavement. Sometimes he would just bite the cold chocolate around them and offer the fruit in the center to his sister. She liked the fruit.

SOME SUMMERS

Some summers Tia and Joey traced the sticky bottom of the El from Frankford to Sixty-Ninth Street on bikes, Rollerblades, New Balances, or brown-and-silver tokens, scraping wads of gum off their bodies and burning up like horny animals darting out of a flaming zoo. Joey scraped his knee; Tia got a scar. There was no telling what they might find out in West Philly or Upper Darby, other people's neighborhoods, other kid's sanctuaries or hellscapes. A boyfriend here, a girlfriend there, a stranger far too old for either of them who had air-conditioning and soft hands and cable TV. They had confidence with no direction. Bad, sad, and horrifying were subjective states of excitement. Sometimes fear, but mostly hype. Who they were way across the city was anyone's guess.

Tia thought it would be a good idea to light a car on fire, but Joey was too scared. Joey thought it would be a good idea to kiss Tia, but she was far past being into that. They snuck into Orleans 8 to watch *Scary Movie*, *X-Men*, and *The Cell* up at Roosevelt Mall, the soles of their sneakers squishing all the way to the front seats like nothing was happening. They scuffled with other kids in the parking lot, throwing rocks and bottles but never quite hitting each other. Joey wondered where they might end up if they kept going, past the Northeast and Holmesburg suburbs, if they could just keep feeling good, if they never stopped moving.

He pulled out a map.

"Boy, where the hell did you even get that?" Tia said.

"Don't worry about it," Joey said. And he pointed to a nondescript section of the map as if he knew where they were going. "Here," he said. "We should go up here."

"Alright, whatever," Tia said.

And they took off again, running in every direction and growing up too fast and too slow to focus on any single thing at once.

It was in middle school at Harding, after they moved into a house down the street from the projects on Glenloch, where Joey's armpits began to grow hair. Chia Pet arms, Tia called them, which Joey did eventually think was kind of funny. And since the two no longer touched, Joey learned to touch himself. When Joey discovered they would all be moving into a house, he couldn't fathom how, always having believed that houses were only for rich people. *Had Popop really hit one of those numbers? Did gold coins come spraying out from a scratch-off, rather than just ten more dollars to buy ten more?* Now, in a house the children had separate rooms, small squares with a window where Joey could, if he wanted, step out onto the roof over a garage. He could hide out in his room all day and play video games but wasn't allowed to lock the door, so anyone might pop in. But the bathroom was different. That was a private space, for pooping or showering or touching oneself without anyone else's permission. Now, it was Joey who was always in the bathroom, sitting on the toilet with his pants pulled down to his ankles, caressing the whole length of his thighs with an abundance of cocoa butter lotion and warming himself to the thought of Jennifer Lopez on the beach in that "Love Don't Cost a Thing" video, wishing he was Jet Li in Aaliyah's "Try Again," and so forth. When *Queen of the Damned* came out, he swore someone had answered his innermost desires for Aaliyah to bite his face off and suck him dry in the middle of a hyped-up half-naked crowd, cheering or running and screaming at the bloodshed.

But touch and hair were only internal changes; it was the external world, as Joey saw it, that was radically transformed in some ways and poisonously similar in others.

Ganny was gone.

Where she had gone wasn't clear to any of the children right away, just that she was no longer with them, replaced as she was by Popop's first love, and Tia's birth mother, Gloria. Everyone called her Dotty. There was a rumor that Dotty had always been a fixture in Popop's life—if not material and fleshy, then at least in the imaginary space of how his life should have gone. The rumor from Tia was that Popop got the house not because it was closer to middle school for Joey, but to lure Dotty back to him. He'd known her before Ganny, and like himself, Dotty was among the few who was able to quit smoking crack in the '90s. They'd had two daughters already, Joey's aunt Tia, and Joey's older aunt, Isha, who lived elsewhere. Dotty had been away, living with an older, light-skinned man while Popop was with Ganny. And while

Popop and Ganny had no children together, Dotty had several light-skinned baby boys with the older light-skinned man, the youngest of whom was named Boo Butt, a terror of a creature that would push Joey to the limits of his sanity. Boo Butt had this gigantic, rock-type head that he didn't mind bashing people with. Joey had been jumped or beaten up outside many times, but he'd never met a child as aggressive as Boo Butt, nor one who seemed to enjoy the pain he inflicted as much. Yet, despite this, and because Boo Butt was smaller and younger than Joey, he had to restrain himself when retaliating for the fear of ending his life.

Boo Butt seemed to take the fact that Joey was taller as a challenge. If Joey was playing video games, he'd grab something heavy and smack him in the face with it while he was off guard. Boo Butt was also quick in joining the long-held tradition of calling Joey a faggot, just when he thought the trend was dying down. He'd jump at Joey, asking him what his bitch ass was gonna do about it, all the while completely aware that his mother, the new queen of the home, had his back. Dotty did, almost as much as Joey felt it appropriate, slap the shit out of Boo Butt and even gave him beatings, but she always took his side first and no punishments ever seemed to matter. He was her baby boy. And perhaps Joey was jealous of this, discovering how much time and effort some mothers seemed to put into their children despite the child's behavior. Boo Butt was around the same age as Joey's younger brother JuJu Man, who, because of his timidness, was often relegated to the background when not being smacked up by Boo Butt.

Mika, for her part, would outright fistfight Boo Butt regularly, certainly to the death if Dotty wasn't there to break it up. That was Dotty's primary import to their household: authority. If there was anyone who didn't play that shit, it was Dotty. In a home where order had always been an afterthought, considered only when an activity annoyed Popop and resulted in a pop to the head or some cursing, Dotty instituted a regime of power that Joey, most of the time, loved.

Despite the roaches that followed them from Paul Street, Dotty would not stand for the stickiness of the floor, the clogginess of the sink, the refrigerator slathered in everything but stuff you could eat. All through the morning, the evening, and the night Dotty could be heard ordering cleanliness or at least the performance of it. All the kids had chores. Joey, Mika, and Tia rotated on kitchen and dish duty; Joey also had the alleyway and the trash, which was a man's job. The performance of these duties grew out of hand, and Joey's most grueling memories therein are of trying to scrub out, wash out, buff out that thickest-of-thick grime on the kitchen floor and the counter and the table that wasn't going anywhere. It felt like the leftover ooze from a gang of aliens had been bottled up and poured out all over the kitchen and clumped and congealed and attracted flies and their babies, whose hatching and cycling through a metamorphosis had overdetermined the filth and the original landscape, however buried under the surface of some linoleum or wood table it might be. The aching of Joey's forearms and back told the repeated story of a failure to unearth some prior state of beauty. It was almost as if Dotty wanted the house, especially the kitchen, to look like her.

Beauty was the trait that Dotty was most known for and the one that Joey was least interested in. But having a hot new ganny wasn't uncomfortable, no matter how many other kids and men and young girls in their neighborhood drew attention to it. She was just Dotty. She was short and thick and appeared very young, like Tia but with a bigger butt, a booty whose particularity on Glenloch Street became legend in the summer, for she strutted out past the fire hydrant in her favorite jean coochie cutters and long black wig switching to death. Whenever asked about her, Joey just said that she was his grandmother and boys of all ages would ask if she was single and if they could fuck her, as if Joey held the keys to his grandmother's coochie and the interest or authority in distributing her goods on demand. The amount of times Joey was asked if that was really his new ganny was far greater than anyone had ever asked if the kids in the house were okay. Dotty, much like Tia, enjoyed a certain kind of subversiveness that Joey thought was funny. If ever Joey was confused about Popop's newfound timidness around or deference to Dotty, she'd have quick explanations.

"Joey, you know I puts it the fuck down. Nigga better watch his mouth if he think he gone keep gettin up in this pussy," she'd say.

Fast-fading were the more timid days of coochie. Dotty's stories about how well she was fucking Popop and how she had him pussy whipped were designed to tell people in and out of the house who she was, who her man was, and how much she and that man loved each other proudly and openly.

She spoke in rapid, long bursts like Popop, too, especially when they argued. Dotty's favorite phrase was *I know you ain't gone leave my goddamn kitchen dirty like that, damn suds all in the sink, fuck wrong wit you, nigga.* Which was second only to: *Earl, I know you don't think I'm like that bitch Ruby, you better not dare lay a hand on me; I will fuck you up.* There was something unfamiliar and pleasant about not having to watch someone get beat down at home all the time. Joey both admired and loathed Dotty. She brought order to a scramble, a mess of internal and external filth that were just normal living standards prior to her arrival and transformation of the household. All the not/hardly showering or brushing teeth or sweeping floors went out the window. Just because you're poor doesn't mean you have to be dirty, too, the kids were told; cleaning, or at least the yelling that preceded the eventual cleaning, took place around the clock. And everyone would be attending school. If you were cutting, you *ain't gone be all the fuck up in this house wit ya lazy ass.*

Mika and Joey argued about Dotty too, taking opposite sides again, perhaps predetermined by how they felt about their own mother. It felt strange for Joey, having to defend her when it was clear she was the better option. Yeah, she was quite annoying and impenetrable when drunk; she shared too much too often, was too touchy and demanding of affection at all times, but she felt, to him, like someone interested in and capable of making things better. And there were few such people around.

"I don't know why you like that bitch so much," Mika said. "She so fuckin crazy."

Tia said little to nothing about her mother, at least not to Joey. And she'd gradually make herself more and more scarce after Dotty's official moving in. There were rumors that Dotty had molested Tia as a child, other arguments between her and Popop that would crop up whenever he really wanted to inflict pain; and to have Dotty tell it, Popop was fuckin or tryna fuck everybody, including "nasty ass Keisha." Joey always wondered to what extent these things were real, but asking about them, or discussing them openly, was off-limits. So Joey assumed it was true, but it was nonetheless confusing because he'd never heard of a woman doing something like that, least of all Dotty who, as mean as she wanted to be sometimes, was nevertheless about her business in every conceivable circumstance. Of course, all men raped and beat people up whenever they got the chance, but Dotty? It was hard to imagine. Joey didn't know how to interpret the silences. And Tia and Dotty would argue a lot. In ways that Joey didn't quite understand, like he was missing something between them, like they had a history that was prior to each moment they spoke but impossible to bring up clearly. Eventually, when Joey was woken up in the middle of the night or had to get up for school in the morning, he stopped looking for Tia around the house at all. At one time they were constant companions, but now, it seemed that Dotty was pushing her away. The dishes would eventually split two ways then, between Mika and himself, now officially being the biggest and the oldest. Whereas Tia had been the person Joey trusted most in the world, his reliance quickly shifted to Dotty.

Remarks about how beautiful Dotty was were never-ending and drowned out most every other dialogue, even Popop's anger. Popop loved the attention she got from teenage boys and how, even though she was a grandmother and mother of four children herself, she still looked and dressed like one of those kids. She walked around the house in heels, hugging everyone, interrupting folks watching TV or playing video games. She stuck out her tongue, all the way to her chin, and said, "Don't I look cute?"

"Yes, Dotty," Joey said, with everyone else murmuring the same. Saying no was rarely an option.

When Dotty grabbed or hugged Mika to get her attention, Mika would yell, "Dotty, get off me! So damn annoying," before shrugging her off and wiping the kiss from her cheek.

Whenever someone didn't go along with the game, Dotty turned to play-fighting until she got the laughs, the hugs, the lipstick on your cheek that represented her love for you and yours for her. Not abiding by these rules would get kids cursed out, as if she'd snapped suddenly out of her drunk-and-happy phase, so it was always better to play along. She'd even become resentful, holding it against someone for days if they didn't hug her or receive the kiss on the cheek while she was drinking, giving them extra chores or making sure they spent as little idle time as possible. If Joey was too tired to deal with her excitement, he'd try to get up and walk away when he saw Dotty coming.

"Nigga don't be walkin around my house all mopey and shit," she'd say, either approaching for tickling or turning to insults if that failed.

Relenting, Joey would say, "Okay, Okay. You got it," laughing when he could.

All the time Dotty grabbed other kids by the arm, pulling them into the kitchen saying, "Look how fuckin clean my kitchen is. Ain't that shit beautiful? That shit sexy, ain't it?" And it was impossible to deny that, despite those fucking roaches, this was the cleanest environment that Joey had ever lived in.

It was easy for Joey to admire Dotty's gumption, her ability to defend herself, and the order that she demanded, but all her interventions were too late. There was something in him, some filth that could not be scraped clean, no matter how hard and how long he might attempt excavation. The sink seemed to embody this conundrum, and Dotty's kitchen was spotless, always. The problem, for Joey at least, was that this was not a kitchen that could be made spotless. It was composed of spots. The stains of everything that lived and died were still there, whether they were spoken of or not; it made him feel crazy, wondering how no one seemed to care, how easily they could pretend that everything was fine.

"My kitchen," Dotty said, "better be the fuck clean." And she meant it. That sink. The word "triflin," Joey thought, must have emerged from the sink between two and three a.m. after the creatures inside scattered apart when the light came on and was known infinitely afterward as the negative adjective for all indescribably vile subjects and actions. The roaches on Glenloch were different from the ones on Paul Street, too. Here, they had more space to roam around, and for some reason they were much better swimmers. There were fewer of them, though they were mostly bigger and more talented and lived longer. Quality over quantity. Less active during the day, they were like an exuberant pack of Gremlins at night, fighting off any humans stepping foot into their territory. Their tiny legs clacked around all night on the countertop, bodies fell to the floor in scrambles; their exoskeletons crunched under Joey's red-and-black Adidas flip-flops as he walked through the sticky beast of a kitchen, hunched over and ready to defend himself.

It wasn't the idea of doing a chore, or the work of cleaning the kitchen that bothered him necessarily, but that such a process was gallivanted around as a higher state of being. Washing dishes and cleaning the kitchen was no big deal. Washing *those* dishes and cleaning *this* kitchen was mortally wounding. Amid the floating chunks of protoplasmic goo there, the Matchbox cars, candy canes, and shoelaces, Joey had found a whole half a chicken skeleton being narrowed down by bacteria, from who knew when. He pulled the slimy chicken skeleton from the water and dragged it into the living room where everyone might be watching *Living Single* or *Martin*.

Holding the chicken skeleton in both hands, Joey would ask, "What is this?"

"Chicken, nigga, what it look like," Popop said.

"Joey, move from in front of the TV," Mika said.

"Boy, get the hell outta here," Dotty said.

Chicken still in hand, dripping the greenish sludge buildup from the sink, Joey squinted at everyone. "Are we for real? Is this real? Who put this whole fucking thing in the sink?"

"Fuck is you cussin at?" Dotty said.

"Joey, get the hell outta here," Popop said.

Then, Joey would turn and walk back into the kitchen, cursing under his breath. "Man, fuck this."

He became obsessed with the fact that someone, at some point, thought the whole chicken should go there, right next to the trash can but not in it. And how often would he have to keep digging his fingernails into the cacophony of bent knives and grease, dead mice and spaghetti noodles, becoming less able to distinguish between any of them? When were these things even prepared and discarded? Who, allegedly, had done the dishes the night before, and left so much detritus, so boldly, so casually? More than not knowing these things, the frustration that Joey felt was based on how everyone called him crazy for bringing it up at all, as if he'd lost his mind for thinking that the sink was not for animal carcasses, whole cans of spinach, and cranberry sauce. Anything could happen in there. But he cleaned it meticulously, leaving nothing alive or wriggling, before finally heading to bed.

Dotty would often wake Mika or Tia or Joey in the middle of the night, especially before school, it seemed, if the kitchen wasn't quite up to her standards.

"Nigga," she said, "getcho ass up and get them motherfuckin suds out my sink! Fuck wrong wit you. This *my* house. I know you ain't leave no fuckin suds in my sink. Get up and rinse that shit out. Up here laying in bed and shit. Yall kids lazy as hell. Got the nerve to leave my kitchen like that. Fuck wrong wit you. You know I don't play that shit."

"Oh my fucking God," Joey mumbled.

"Fuck you say?" Dotty said.

"Nothing," Joey said. "Nothing."

"Oh, I fuckin thought so," Dotty said.

Then, groggy, Joey got up and sagged downstairs, shaking his head. Upon gazing at the kitchen sink, he always thought, *I know she ain't wake me up at 3:30 to rinse out this dollop of soap.*

Harding Middle School was right next to Red Brick Projects and just two blocks away from where the family now lived. Before Joey's first day, Popop and Dotty acted like he should be excited, but he couldn't understand why. By then, he'd already come to hate school so much that the thought of being in any building designated as such repulsed him. He would do it, of course, because he had to graduate and get a job so that he could move and never talk to anyone he knew ever again, but he wasn't going to walk around acting happy about the process. The only good thing he perceived about the change was that no one knew him yet at this new school.

He was even lankier now, which made him appear thinner. Joey had gained at least a foot in height, and to his knowledge was the only one in middle school who could dunk, despite his fear of doing so in public. While taking the trash out in the morning before walking the short distance over to the school, he considered that one day, being able to dunk might earn him some respect. Though he couldn't figure out why, already, he was crying before stepping foot inside of the new building. He lined up all the trash bags with holes next to each other first, then the sealed bags, then the trash cans without bags in them, then the trash cans with bags to establish a hierarchy. It was always trash day. He noticed a few people gathered in the empty lot across the street from his house with wild grass everywhere. That same lot was where, in the summer, Joey would watch praying mantises gather to have sex. He wanted to see what was going on but couldn't spare the time and was worried that he might be late to school and draw attention to himself.

In his sheared blue New Balances, he stomped through condoms and weave braids, kitchenware and cherry water ice cups from Rita's on his way to school, cutting his toes on a sliced-open Big Gulp Slurpee from 7-Eleven—it was a wound that would take weeks to heal—Philly blunt wrappers and flaming hot Cheetos getting lodged inside, the sting like a wasp each time his foot dropped, all the junk pulling him down into nothing. But it was nice out. He walked slowly to school because he knew it was just as terrifying, perhaps a little more, than it had always been. The thought of being around other boys made him tremble and created the urge to pee. He kept thinking that he would change something this time; he would act instead of simply being acted upon.

He had already taken some measures, of course. He was working on his hair. What he had was always affectionately called "that nigga shit," but he'd noticed how all the boys started wearing du-rags and stocking caps and using the thick can of Murray's to grow waves like Usher in the "You Make Me Wanna" video. So Joey did, too. Du-rags were only a dollar and Popop already had Murray's around all the time, heating up on the radiator. So, Joey went to work. He stopped washing his hair so often, instead oiling it up every night before tying his black du-rag on tight and then regreasing it every morning and trying to rub out the lined indentation it made into his forehead. He started to get lumps on his head, too, little white pimples around where the du-rag exerted pressure and big boils on the back of his dome that hurt, but it was fine because he also started to get waves; some nights he'd stand in front of the mirror and burst the pustules open, squealing in pain, but also relieved from the popping. He wanted to like himself, and this was helping. He had something that other boys had that he also thought was attractive; he could—as long as he didn't smile—look at himself in the mirror for more than a few seconds without getting sad, running his fingers along the top of his head, feeling the rise and fall of the black ocean that he and Murray's built.

This was what he did with his hands on the way to school. He brushed and rubbed, brushed and rubbed with a wooden brush he kept—like all the other short-haired boys who wanted to be Usher and for girls to like it their way—in that mini cargo pocket of his khakis, those imitation Dickies that were part of the school uniform. Shitty, uneven haircut from Popop or not, at least the waves were tight. He could feel them.

So many of the other kids at Harding seemed like they were already grown, especially the girls, whose bodies were shaped like the women Joey saw on the Box, or like Pam from *Martin*, like his own new ganny, Dotty. The tiny desks and style of instruction seemed insulting to everyone's size and demeanor, even his own. And somehow, hierarchies had already been established between and among every grade and gender in school before things got started. Teachers said things, but Joey was too afraid to hear any of it, watching other kids watch him, adjusting his posture, being sure not to smile or look at anyone's face directly, pushing away any trembling and so forth. A light-skinned boy named Damien was in charge of all the boys. He was mad chubby with long hair and straight teeth; he smiled a lot. Joey swore he was twenty. And in every class, he seemed to have different girls braiding or playing in his hair as he shot spitballs at people's faces or at teachers when they turned around. He cursed and got in and out of his seat whenever he wanted to give someone dap or talk shit about their clothes. He was surrounded by other boys, too, who came in and out of class at odd times or hung out in front of the school smoking.

Damien also had a sister named Ebony, who was so fine that Joey damn near stumbled every time he saw her. He thought she must have been high school aged already. She was as tall as him but thick, and always had long box braids; her legs took up most of her body, always in those pants with no back pockets that made her butt look rounder. Ebony was brown-skinned and always wore a smirk that suggested she might laugh or knock some other girl's or boy's teeth out at any moment. Sometimes she did. The worst part was that whenever she walked by Joey in the halls, she would rub the side of her butt against him and smile, turning her head back to look at him, lifting up one of her cheeks. There was a game indicated here that the kids used to play where all the boys would chase girls around and smack them on the ass, and so the halls were normally filled with children running around and squealing and laughing and ending up in bathrooms together later.

But Ebony was not one of those girls who played this game. At all. One of the boys approached her once, just gesturing like he was gonna slap her ass, and the look she gave him inflicted literal pain on every surrounding party. He withdrew, only for Ebony to grind him up about his highwaters in class the next day when he sat down and the bottom of his pants no longer reached his sneakers. Joey watched this in awe, sagging his own pants before sitting, desperate to make them reach his feet. It was the first time Joey had seen another boy who was supposedly cool just sit there and cry as Ebony stood over him pointing out everything fucked-up about his clothes, his body, his lacking intellect, his "little baby dick" that "aint ready" for her pussy anyway, his weak ass hangtime, his weird ass body that was wide up top and skinny from the waist down; she went in on his voice, which "sound like a white girl getting fucked in a porno," she said. The whole thing was rough, and the classroom was in an uproar as the teacher sat behind her desk reading a newspaper. He eventually walked out of class that day, and didn't really regain any respect until, at the urging of Damien, he beat some random sixth-grade boy with glasses so bad he had to go to the hospital, after which Joey couldn't remember seeing the kid again. To Joey's surprise, even after all this, yet another boy eventually lifted his hand with the suggestion that he was gonna slap Ebony's ass from the top, but she turned around and just straight jabbed him in the mouth, busted his lip and everything. People never stopped laughing about it.

Joey wanted to touch Ebony's butt. So. Damn. Badly. But even more so than touching, he wanted Ebony to ask him to touch her butt, to just get him alone and put his hand there and wherever else. Everywhere else. But while she looked and smelled like a grown ass black woman—all meticulously soaped, oiled, and lotioned—she definitely fought like a high school girl. Boys, girls, anyone, she would square up and punch their faces in, slam heads to the ground by hair, and talk shit just as well as Tia could, but louder. Whenever Ebony's hair slid across Joey's arm in the hall, he imagined her lotioning up her whole body butt naked after the shower before she put any clothes on, absolutely proud of every inch of herself.

So many times, Ebony passed Joey in the halls, and he would start to open his mouth, to almost say something, and she'd stop and pause for a second in anticipation, expectant until, met with the minor disappointment of Joey's silence, she'd walk off with her friends laughing, not at him, but maybe at the fact of, what seemed to her, his unnecessary shyness. But Joey did grow bolder as time went on at school. He stayed under the radar more broadly, allowing kids who looked goofier or were less savvy than him to take the brunt of social punishment. He began diverting the jokes at his own person by laughing along with the crowd or developing an intense sarcasm in his most frustrated moments, deflecting with an obscurity that no one understood, but with a tone that always suggested playing the shit out of the other person. It wasn't long before an exchange with Ebony in the hallway might look like this:

"Hey, Ebony, what's up?"

"Oh, nothing," Ebony would say, sliding a hand onto Joey's flat chest. "What you tryna do?"

"You know," Joey would say. "Just tryna get to this dumb ass class."

Progress. Not quite smooth, but it was the opening of a line of inquiry with an older girl who, Joey swore, under the right conditions, would be into him. On the rare occasions he spoke to Tia, she told Joey that *What you tryna do?* was about fucking and he was too slow to catch on. And Joey wanted to believe this but wasn't quite confident enough. *Why wouldn't she just say it directly if that's what she wanted? Surely she has all the words and little of the fear,* Joey thought, *to talk about that kind of stuff, so why the code?* Joey knew that people ducked away into the bathrooms at Harding all the time to have sex, but it seemed like a real official thing that he wasn't sure he was ready for. Just in case, however, he did ask Popop for a condom, which the older man only too excitedly handed him. A golden ticket, they called the Trojan Magnums back then, which, even if Joey wasn't about to "go out and get him some real pussy," like Popop said, he was still just happy for the fact that his winkey, now an official penis, or dick, depending on the conversation, had grown to a condom-fitting size.

Progress.

He'd even felt progress with smothering himself enough so that other boys wouldn't notice how truly afraid and uncomfortable he was. He could nod his head, give dap, laugh along, run fast, wash his body, keep his distance, look away, look down, sit alone, keep quiet, and reply, without ever missing a beat to inquiries like "You good?" with a swift "Yeah, we good, man," and nothing else. But. There was a time when Joey's hallway flirtations with Ebony must have given something away, must have betrayed a sense that he wanted more than just to touch and fuck her, but to hold and be with her in a way that he heard other boys constantly refer to as gay, weak, or soft, all interchangeable words at Harding. It was a fatal mistake to be outed as sensitive, or soft on some girl, to long for anything or anyone in such a way that the word "longing" might fit the description. Damien approached Joey after noticing the intensity of his desire in one of those short exchanges with Ebony.

"Hey, wassup, young boul," he said, reaching out to shake Joey's hand. And since this wasn't their first exchange, Joey knew that Damien knew his name by now, but he would never say it, and only refer to him as a young boul.

Joey reached his hand out to return the gesture, but before their hands met, Damien pulled his own hand away.

"Syke!" he shouted, pulling back and reaching into his hair.

Damien's crew gathered around him and laughed, and this was when Joey knew he'd fucked up. It was over. Any anonymity and fake cool he'd tried to project from day one had been exposed, not only because it was clear that he wanted to love up on Ebony, but because he also longed to be accepted, to be liked by Damien and other boys, at least enough that they might refer to him by his name. Something in his body gave all this away no matter how much he tried to hide it.

Later that day, Joey was sitting in the cafeteria eating his lunch alone. He'd waited all day for that boat-shaped pizza and bag of chocolate milk. Hot cheese and sauce always hit the spot, helped him forget about things if only for the moment of eating. Even the sides of stiff, unseasoned green beans felt precious, having sat or slept through nonsensical lectures all day about every kind of matter that was not his own. At the long lunch table, he was facing away from the lunch line behind him, so excited about eating that he'd neglected to find a place where his back was to the wall. And then, at the very moment of lapsed caution, the coldest smack in the history of smacks came across the back of his head.

"Open neck, no respec, bitch nigga!" yelled Rashaid. He was one of the boys who hung with Damien, almost as tall as Joey and dark-skinned with a small Afro that was aspiring to braid length.

The cafeteria erupted in laughter and long, drawn-out *daaaaaamn*s. The echo of the open space that was also the gym on Wednesdays didn't help. It was everything that Joey feared but knew would happen. But he also knew what he should do this time. He darted to his feet, facing the boy who'd just hit him. The lunchroom grew silent and attentive to the whole encounter then. Joey was, for some reason, still holding his lunch tray, too. He stepped closer to Rashaid, all up in his face, and took a deep breath. He had to respond differently now. Everything was on the line, and he was doing his best not to cry. He closed his eyes for just a second, deciding what to do with his body, how to hurt the boy so this would never happen again. Then, Damien stepped forward and slapped Joey's food tray to the ground.

"Fuck outta here, little faggot ass nigga," he said. "You ain't about shit."

The lunchroom started laughing again, but this time was a little different. There were some people, certainly not the majority, who felt a little bad, disgusted even. Joey could hear some of them sighing, even over the laughter. They took pity on him and the whole situation in a way that broke Joey's spirit like never before.

That's a shame, other kids said. *They don't gotta mess with that little boy like that.*

Kids still sitting at the tables shook their heads in pity, died laughing, or just kept eating as Joey stood there with Rashaid's finger in his face, poking at his nose as the other boy kept saying "What pussy?" over and over again. The head shaking and moans of those people who actually pitied him, including the lunch security guard, were too much to bear. Fat tears rolled down Joey's face. "What, pussy?" Rashaid poked him in the forehead.

"Little bitch cryin, too," he said. Then, he turned to address the whole lunchroom, still with one finger poking Joey's forehead. "These faggot niggas soft as shit out here!"

Joey was hyperventilating when Rashaid's palm, softly, grabbed Joey's face before thrusting it down and away, effectively sitting him back down.

"That's how we fuckin do!" Rashaid said. "We mug these bitch ass niggas."

Joey, now having been pushed back into his seat, looked down at the smeared pizza on his uniform pants. Rashaid and Damien walked off laughing. Then Joey got up and left the cafeteria in silence, trying to avoid everyone's eyes, especially Ebony and the older girls.

At home, Joey locked himself inside his room and tried to play video games but just couldn't. They were no fun anymore; he couldn't stop thinking about the next day, about going to school and coming home, going to school and coming home, about having to interact with other people in any way at all. The names that Popop called him from the other side of the door didn't matter; the kitchen was a waste of time; he couldn't eat or think or focus on the joy he might squeeze out of fantasies where he might otherwise embed himself. He knew that nothing would change on its own, and so he sat in darkness, and silence, past dinner and chores, just working up the courage to try something else.

Past the naivete of asking for help in his personal affairs, Joey decided to take matters into his own hands. Patience was in no way a virtue, and there was no telling what his spirit or emotional capacity might corrode into while just sitting around and waiting for something to happen or get better. Therefore, there would be no more snitching and getting jumped, no more letting Popop know and being hit and berated by him too, and no longer would he share information with anyone else to be teased; no, he was done with all of that. What he could do, though, was kill. Supposedly Popop had tried to kill someone before and no one ever bothered him afterward; the boys at school talked shit that Damien had murdered another boy before; that big light-skinned drug dealer who pulled the gun on Joey a block away, who was trying to have sex with Mika, had killed someone before; it seemed the only reasonable way to be free of the constant belittling and violence was to prove that he was willing to end someone else's life once and for all.

There was a box cutter in Popop's room that Joey knew was very sharp. He'd accidentally cut himself with it before, trying to open up an unusually stiff pack of orange slices. The blade slid clean through Joey's pointer finger with little effort, so he could imagine what it might do to someone's face or neck given enough force. This excited him. Popop had so many box cutters accidentally left in his pockets from work that he wouldn't notice just one of them missing, either. Joey grabbed it while fetching Popop a beer from the mini fridge. He tested the blade out on his own finger, poking the sharp part out just a little and dabbing himself to draw blood. Then, he practiced taking the silver blade out of his pocket and flicking it open smoothly and quickly enough to do what he needed. Over and over again, he put away and withdrew the blade, put it away and then withdrew it again, becoming defter as he went on. He thought about piercing the thin skin of another boy's neck and how much pressure it might take, right below the Adam's apple as he cut through the thick layer of fascia at the bottom of his mattress, slowly, dragging the blade from one end to another.

The long spaghetti noodle of a nothing that was Joey would demand, once and for all, that he become something, whatever that thing was. Social standing be damned, he would decide what was good and what was not and who could sit and eat where or be left alone and when. On the morning in question, Joey carried the box cutter to school in his right pocket. He kept one hand on the blade the whole time, ready to flip it open at a moment's notice, lest anyone decide that it was time to touch him for any reason whatsoever. This would be the day that Rashaid died, and no one would feel sorry for it.

Or maybe they would.

Joey pictured how Rashaid would be valorized by everyone they knew, the same boy who he'd seen punch girls in the face like Popop punched Ganny, who he imagined would one day be just another Popop if left to his own devices. He considered that, from the perspective of his family and community, Rashaid was just a troubled youth trying to make it, doing his best, and Joey, well, he was a shiftless nerd bloating with self-importance, a crybaby who, instead of learning how to toughen up and fight for himself, decided, like the sissy he was, to take an innocent boy's life like he was some kind of God. Certainly, Rashaid's mother, like so many of the other boys' mothers Joey knew, loved him. Certainly, she worked a myriad of jobs to keep her little boy happy after big Rashaid fled or died or went to jail. Certainly, Joey would be ashamed and shamed for what he was about to do to someone's pure and oh-so-sweet baby boy. So be it. He had long since passed the shallow threshold of good and evil, right and wrong, violence or not. It was all violence, it was all wrong, and it was all he could do to lay claim to his own body. If being a good person meant laying down for even a second longer, then it was not something he could ever aspire to. *Fuck it then*, Joey thought. Let the R.I.P. Rashaid shirts fly and the creepy loner, loser comments about himself follow; at least he would have permanently corrected one problem the only way he knew how.

He waited.

All through school on the assigned day, Joey watched Rashaid from the corner of his eye, desperate to see him put his head down or fall asleep in the period before last. It was part of his routine. Joey had gotten so accustomed to knowing everyone's patterns by then, which side of the hall they walked on, which foot they put forward first, where they were most likely to sit, when they'd be outside smoking. He suddenly realized how much energy this took up, paying so much attention to everyone else just to hide from them, but it was also useful now for what he wanted to do.

By the time Rashaid was nodding off toward the end of the day, Joey could hardly wait. He thumbed the box cutter in his pocket, sliding the blade in and out, cutting the inside of his pants a little. The teacher was reading a newspaper after she handed out a worksheet that sat empty on most of the kids' desks, or turned into paper airplanes, spitballs, or grotesque artworks. Joey got up without revealing his blade and slid the end of it out his pocket as he walked toward Rashaid. He rehearsed this so many times over in his head. He would reach for the boy's neck and slice right across, hard and deep; it wouldn't be nearly as thick as a tree trunk, and the blood would spill immediately. Then, Joey would sit back down like nothing happened. He was trembling. But it wasn't the trembling of nervousness; he was excited. He hadn't been this excited in so long, and he walked slow and deliberately, trying to hide the joy.

But before he could even reach the other boy, the school's fire alarm went off. Joey assumed, at first, that it was just another joke. The same kids who pulled the fire alarm any other time were pulling the fire alarm now, and he could get to his seat and wait for it to be over. But this was different. The teacher went out into the hallway and came back pale. He'd seen the teacher afraid before, but of the students. Not like this.

"We're evacuating the building," she said.

For what? Joey thought. *The alarm goes off all the time.* But the fear in the teacher's eyes then was different. Joey recognized it as the same kind of fear he'd felt in himself day in and day out, in and out of school.

After being gathered outside without any real information for about an hour, all the kids got sent home early. Some parents even came to gather their children from the front of the building, crying and rushing them into cars or running back home with them. Rashaid's mother came to get him, hugging and kissing and crying all over him before shuffling him into a brand-new-looking Acura. Joey's heart stopped thumping as hard then, and he looked around as he felt it slowing down. He had not killed Rashaid, nor had he been hit that day, either, and now he was being sent home early from school. Even the urge to kill another boy began receding amid the confusion. All the nerve Joey had worked up in himself started to peel off his body. Was he even sure he could've done it? The shame of organizing this plan in the first place hit him hard on the walk home, pouring out as the adrenaline left. What in the world was he thinking? And why was he thinking about it so often?

When he walked in the front door, Dotty asked what the hell he was doing home so early, suggesting that he had better not be cutting school.

"No, Dotty, I don't even know," he said. "They just sent us home."

"For fuckin what?" She asked.

He knew nothing.

There was still commotion across the street in the empty lot where the praying mantises came, but now there were cops. They had found a dead man who had been raped and killed; the open brown of his body left roasting in the sun.

When Popop came home a little early, everyone knew something must have been really wrong. A plane had crashed into a building in New York and on television people were losing it.

Popop was unimpressed. "They sent yall home early for that?" he said. "That's all the fuckin way over there. Coulda kept y'all asses in school. Messin wit my money and shit, too."

Nearly needless to say, Joey eventually decided that school was not for him. Luckily, though, being a punk meant that his behavior, at least at Harding et al., was enough to float him by with passing grades. Just coming to class on occasion and not threatening the teachers or "being disruptive" could earn anyone a B; keeping one's guard up was enough of an energy drain as it was. But there was a problem: he could not cut school and sneak around at home anymore. Dotty was there, and she simply didn't play that. Joey needed a new approach, which started with just wandering around.

Alone, Joey didn't look like a child, at least heightwise, and so he was hardly bothered by cops hunting for truants. When they did approach him, the worst they would do was curse and tell him to take his ass to school. Joey got a basketball and strolled around during the day to courts that were empty so he could practice shooting and dunking. It felt good to be alone and to get to know his body in another way, without the fear of someone else watching or the demand to satisfy things outside his own curiosity. He became a staple resident at one of the smaller courts in North Philly, acting like he wasn't trying to show off for all the grown women walking by with strollers or small children asking why he wasn't in school.

"I aint no kid," he said. "I look that young?" He began lying compulsively about his age.

They always laughed or rolled their eyes. Sometimes, if they had children who could walk but weren't school aged yet, Joey would play with them, performing crossovers and trying to show them how to dribble. They shared cherry water ice from the corner store down the street and licked their fingers clean afterward, dirt and all.

There was one woman, in particular, who lived right across the street from the park in one of those row homes where you could walk right into the basement or the living room through two different doors. Her name was Faye. She was taller than Joey with a black wig and wore thick denim jeans even when it was really warm and spoke softly to him. Once they started chatting regularly, Faye would bring all kinds of food out to Joey and they'd sit on the park bench eating: collard greens with pork neckbones, pasta with white sauce and jumbo shrimp, fried chicken wings and livers and gizzards and rice with kidney beans.

Joey and Faye got to talking about other things they enjoyed, too, and one day it turned to anime. Joey hadn't seen *Blood: The Last Vampire* yet and Faye was appalled.

"Oh my God, boy!" she said. "Never?"

"No, is it really that good?" Joey asked. He was too excited about the prospect but didn't want to let it show.

"Well, just come over," Faye said. "And we can watch it. We got plenty of other ones, too."

Joey realized that this was what he'd wanted her to say all along. And of her husband? Lots of people had one of those. And Faye told Joey he was at work anyway, even longer than Joey was supposed to have been at school. Plus, there was a separate entrance, so if he came home early Joey could just leave from the basement door.

It was brighter in Faye's basement than Joey would have thought, and much cleaner. Two of those thick glass windows faced the street and the sun, so that if she didn't block them, light poured right onto the couch they sat on. It was the first time Joey had seen a finished basement. There was a carpet too, and a really big plasma-screen TV, even bigger than the one that was in Joey's living room back on Paul Street. When they walked in Joey remained standing and looking around perhaps more than was normal, which made Faye laugh.

"You know you can sit down, right?" she said, looking over at the couch.

"Oh yeah. Duh," he replied.

Faye offered him something to drink, and even though he was mad thirsty, Joey said he didn't want anything, but Faye went upstairs and brought down two cups of water anyway. The upstairs, Joey would learn, was off-limits, but he always tried to imagine what her kitchen, where she made the foods they ate on the park bench, was like.

Joey never saw any roaches in Faye's house. Did being in a happy marriage, as hers was often described, mean that you just wouldn't have to deal with roaches? Joey must have been lost in thought that first time over Faye's house because she kept asking him if he was okay. After she covered the windows with dark towels so that the sun wouldn't get in, she sat down next to Joey on the couch again, their bodies more than touching.

"Oh," she said, "I forgot." Before she jumped up to put the movie on.

Joey eyed her as she walked away and leaned over the DVD player without bending her knees. Then Faye came and sat next to, almost on top of Joey again. He was trying not to get hard too quickly, but she knew.

She giggled this time before asking, "You okay?"

"Yeah, I'm good," Joey said, smooth.

Faye put Joey's arm around her, and he pulled her in closer to his body, laid one of her legs over his lap. She laughed at times during *Blood: The Last Vampire* that seemed completely inappropriate, since, while the film was amazing, Joey found absolutely no humor in it. Saya was not fucking around. She ripped grotesque vampires to pieces like breathing but she never smiled or joked with them. And much to Joey's dismay, she never killed any of the cops. But this was less important than the fact that Faye was rubbing on Joey's dick from outside his pants, so sweetly, and so gently, and he felt like he might explode. When he caught himself breathing way too heavy, Faye was staring at him.

She laughed again. "Can I go down on you?" she said.

Joey had never considered that someone might flat-out and directly ask a question like that. It indicated that she wanted to, but it was very different from how he imagined this happening. Didn't people just do and never say? In his mind there was supposed to be a more subtle interplay of bodies, a push and pull and a lot of guesswork, which, while it gave him intense anxiety, was just the way that people had done it. That Faye would even ask was a strange but welcome endeavor, and Joey wondered why it wasn't always like this.

He tried to calm down first before saying yes. He didn't want his voice to crack and betray his age, or to make it seem like he'd never been in this situation before. He kept nodding his head but that wasn't enough; she just stared at him and rubbed. It wasn't until he said yes clearly enough that she un-buttoned his pants and wouldn't let him help, either. Whenever he'd reach out to her she'd swat his hands down and pin them to the couch before moving his right hand to the back of her head. Joey considered himself wise in his years for knowing that sucking penis and eating coochie were necessary forms of foreplay, and that he should not terminate the encounter by prematurely ejaculating into his new girlfriend's mouth right away. His plan was to enjoy what was happening now, then to eat Faye out, and then, after putting on the condom that he had in his back pocket, to have sex with Faye in at least three standard positions: missionary, girl on top, and of course, doggie style. They would start with the fundamentals.

While Faye licked on Joey, he tried to reach down to touch

her coochie but she swatted his hand away again, then pushed herself up onto the couch to kiss him.

"Just let me do it," she said, their cheeks side by side.

But Joey was too insecure about not doing anything for her. When Faye led Joey's hand to linger on her thigh, he slid up between her legs, and there was more material than he'd imagined. He figured then that she must have been on her period and was wearing a hefty pad. Not that the blood would have bothered him, but maybe it would bother her, or she was used to being with people for whom blood was a problem. With this he backed off and tried to just enjoy what she offered, trembling as he came, and she never stopped until he went completely soft. When she was done, Faye went into the bathroom and came out with a hot washcloth to wipe Joey's dick off. It was him, then, who wondered on about her.

"Are you okay?" he said.

And she found this funny, too, but Joey couldn't understand why, after what had just happened. He felt like he was subjecting her to some kind of torture, like he forced her to do something with no benefit and he wanted, desperately, to make it right. But he didn't know how.

"I'm great, baby," she said. "Why wouldn't I be?"

Joey started spending more time at Faye's house when he cut school, which was often. They watched AMVs and debated anime battles: Kenshin vs. Saito, Cell vs. Gohan, Deathscythe vs. Wing Zero, Wing Zero vs. Everyone, and so on, mixing and matching worlds and characters at their leisure. They must have watched *Gundam Wing: Endless Waltz* a million times, swooning and crying over the ending sequence and how the song "White Reflection" made all the difference, and even though they understood none of the words they sang along as if their lives depended on it. But how, in a rebellion led by a seven-year-old child, did the Gundam Pilots manage to stop Operation Meteor without killing a single person? That was bullshit, both Faye and Joey agreed, since any time you destroy a mobile suit, it must be near impossible not to kill the pilot because half of them explode or get discarded in deep space. They imagined that, with the "no murder this time" logic, perhaps someone came by and scooped up pilots from downed suits right after every conflict and there was some Geneva Conventions–type rule everyone pretended to follow.

But when Faye and Joey weren't talking, she was touching or going down on him. And even though Joey grew dependent on Faye's touch, he also got increasingly frustrated as a permanent recipient, a receiver, but never a giver of any affection. In his mind, these limitations were either a boundary that she was keeping up because she had someone, like many girls Joey would end up with, or there was something about him that she didn't want, maybe from inadequacy or lack of desire. It was Joey now always asking if she was okay, or if he could touch her, and when she relented, he realized that she wasn't wearing a pad or anything, but that below her waist was banded and her small bra was stuffed. *Oh!* Joey thought, *I'm a fucking idiot*. It made sense that if Faye was trans she might feel uncomfortable because most people would try to beat her up or kill her. Even in middle school this was obvious; nearly every boy he knew went on about how they would murder anyone who was "really a man" or "tried to trick them," unprompted and angry, always. This was confusing because how could you be tricked into something that you actually wanted with somebody's body that you actually wanted?

Confusion amplified Joey's guilt. He didn't want to start a conversation that would make Faye feel like he was one of those boys that wanted to kill her, nor did he want to make her feel like she had to be with him in some ways that she might not be with her husband. What kind of things did she do with her husband? Joey had no idea. Was it strange that he wanted to watch them have sex to know what he should do?

And then, one day, before Joey could even work up the nerve to start a more detailed conversation about their relationship, Faye's husband came home too early.

He was huge. And although he came through the main door into the living room, he could somehow tell right away that someone else was in the house.

"Babe?" he said all too loud as soon as he walked in. "Where you at?"

Joey supposed that it wasn't normal for Faye to just hang out in the basement alone and that he was about to get the worst ass whooping of his life if he didn't get out fast. His winkey was still hard as he tried to fasten his pants too quickly, but it was like his body could hardly move. He was uncoordinated. Faye yelled upstairs and started moving right away, doing her best to put the man at ease.

"I'm coming!" she said.

"Why you down there?" he said, walking toward the basement stairs.

And that was it. Joey could see his work boots at the top of the steps, and he must have been able to see or smell or hear something because he came darting down the basement steps faster than Joey could move. Maybe he wanted to get caught, because how could he not have made it out of the basement door quick enough? It didn't matter. Fates were sealed.

Faye put a hand over her face. "Wait," she said.

"What the fuck?" the man said. "What the fuck is this?"

Her husband was bewildered, his eyes round and bulging, sweat dripping from his forehead and on his shoulders, glistening brown contrasting against his white tank top. Joey couldn't look at him. And in what felt like a forever silence where they all heard each other breathe, her husband's tone shifted into sadness before speaking again.

"Why is this little ass boy in here, Faye?" he said. "What the fuck is this little ass boy doin in here, Faye?" Then he took a deep breath. This time he was definitely talking to Joey. "Young boul," he said. "Get the fuck outta my house."

It took everything Joey had in him to move. Faye was crying. And he felt like he should defend her, but he rose from the couch and sulked away, right out the basement door. Joey's blood congealed at the fact that he could not hear them yelling after he walked out. He imagined that Faye's husband would kill her. He knew it. And he also knew that he would do nothing about it. He walked home slow and sick at having done nothing, at having been nothing for anyone again.

Joey never went to that same park or that part of North Philly again. Even strolling through the area later in life would resurface the guilt. But in the present, going back to school on a regular basis was still out of the question. He might show up once or twice a week, thrice at best, but never for a whole day, moving through the homes of other grown girls as often as necessary. The best times were when most of the older boys were out of class and he could hope they might never return, until they did. And there were metal detectors now, with a security guard, so that even if he worked up the gumption for the box cutter again, it was impossible.

One day he turned to make the sacrificial walk back into Harding Middle School, and Joey discovered that at least three of the boys he was afraid of had been expelled. He didn't care why. It was like now he didn't know anyone there and they didn't know him, and no one really cared to know, either. He would just slide on through what was left of middle school staring at all the substitute teachers reading their newspapers while he doodled in a black notebook at the back of the class. Giant sea creatures and tiny islands, splintering boats and lonely survivors. He'd gotten better, though, moving on to whole anime scene replications, too.

One of his classmates, another black boy Joey's age, strolled to the back trying to mind his business, eyeing his drawing from every angle.

"Fuck kinda gay ass shit is that?" the boy said, drawing attention from the rest of the class.

And without thinking, Joey got up and grabbed the boy by the face, throwing him to the ground as hard as he could. One of the desks fell over. The teacher hopped to his feet and tried to hold Joey back. What he could have done. Joey screamed, his voice cracking every other syllable, choking him, slamming him, kicking him, clawing him.

"I will fuckin kill you!" he said. "Think I'm playin. I will kill ya bitch ass! I dare you to get the fuck up. I will fucking kill you!"

And the teacher tried to soothe the boy like they knew each other, whisper-yelling at him, "You don't need to act like them, just calm down. Just calm down. You don't need to act like them." Joey cursed the teacher, too, wrestling the older man off him.

"Get the fuck off me, dickhead! Don't fuckin touch me," he said. "You and this dumb fuckin school aint shit. None of yall aint shit! I will fucking kill all of you," he said, burning his own throat, burning up all over, and crying.

SOME SUMMERS

Some summers, or rather, one summer positioned as the grand finale of all summers, Joey's mother returned with a man. The kids almost couldn't believe it. Not the man, but that she'd returned at all to fulfill a long-forgotten promise. She had arrived to take back her kids. Keisha was plump and seemed happier than normal, her newfound roundness accentuated by a joy that made Joey uncomfortable in both its fragility and newness. She smiled and hugged the kids like she'd never left, pulling them into her breasts with vigor.

"I missed yall so much!" she said.

Joey and Mika stared at each other while the smaller JuJu Man frolicked around querying who this woman they called Mom was.

The man's name was Moon. He was a bit older than Keisha and much paler. Through no interest of his own, Joey would discover that he was also an Evangelical Christian. Only now did Joey realize that his own family had been Baptist this whole time, and suddenly this meant something to them other than going to church on occasion. There would have been beef with Moon were he not hailed as responsible for turning Keisha's life around and evacuating the kids. "Ya new dad," Popop called him. And Joey was fine with this, as long as he was getting the hell out of Frankford.

Moon and Keisha met in rehab or smoking and fell "instantly in love," as Keisha described it. Tia said this probably just meant that Moon had a big dick, which, by looking at him, since he did seem rather healthy, might have been true. Moon lived in Croydon, which sounded just as real to Joey as an enchanted forest, but that was where his house was and that was where the kids packed up to head out to. The man's car was clean. It smelled like leather and seemed to have never been smoked in. Joey could hardly remember being in a car other than Moon's, and yet he was somehow repulsed by an endless experience of roving cigarette compartments posing as such. Moon didn't drink, either. There would be none of that in his Croydon home, which felt like hundreds of miles away, much farther than Joey and Tia could have ever adventured to, with or without their bikes or the train. The whole ride over, Keisha smiled back at her children, explaining to them how much they were going to love it there.

Moon's house was a one-story building with a dusty basement on a quiet street that felt like no humans were allowed to live there or make their presence known. The people that Joey could see, and only rarely, were older white people who waved and smiled at him as they mowed their lawns. It seemed like everyone had a lawn in Croydon and no fences. Moon had a big backyard that wrapped around the small house with an inconspicuous mound of sand and a tiny pond in the back. Upon seeing this, Joey had already made his plans for an animal sanctuary and enlisted Mika, much to her own excitement, in organizing the outdoor terrarium. They dug out the sand, which was actually a giant anthill, and made as wide a sand border as they could find stretching out from the little pond as a focal point, because every society needs a water source. To build their animal farm, Joey and Mika gathered worms, potato bugs, ants, and millipedes, and on several occasions tried and failed to catch small mammals that they didn't recognize. There were no roaches yet.

This didn't stop the centipedes, though. The inside of Moon's house was centipede heaven, or hell, depending on one's perspective. The walls, once white, were slathered in spots of legs and guts because Joey made it his mission to hunt down and murder every one of them after he'd woken up with one tickling the side of his face and was so startled that he had to forgo sleep that night. Moon and Keisha thought it was strange that Joey was outside playing with bugs all the time but was all of a sudden afraid of slugs and centipedes, while Joey thought it was strange that his mother was suddenly interested in reading anything, let alone a Bible, and even more so that they expected him to be interested in it, too. They were at an impasse. Joey never said, "Fuck outta here," like he wanted to at the suggestion that he should read the Bible, but he did end up reading it in secret, out of his own interest, and, like with many other books he was supposed to have read for school, he didn't find it the least bit interesting.

Life in Croydon was essentially a short loop of fake pleasantries. Or at least they felt fake to Joey, and he could recognize the falsehoods in his mother's temperament too often, the closed-offness of her gestures alongside gentle speech she'd never otherwise use. It felt like she was performing for Moon while Moon was performing for his God. Since when was she asking if Joey was okay, or if the kids were hungry? It seemed more genuine when Moon said it, but that was only because Joey didn't actually know him and assumed he was one of those people silly enough to believe that the world was a naturally kind. Moon's naivete might be genuine, but certainly not his mother's. He knew better than that. But maybe her performance was worth it; the other men she had been with, the black men, all beat her up without exception. One of them, this man named Terrence with a receding hairline, shoved her down a whole flight of stairs, and she acted like it wasn't that bad. So maybe it was worth faking it with Moon.

And Joey had to admit that one of the reasons he didn't like Moon was because there was no playing video games in Croydon. This was completely unacceptable. Sure, it was nice to go outside and be relatively safe, but there was no balance between that safety and absolute monotony. There are only so many pill bugs and sand forts in the world before the hunger for more sets in. But Joey hardly argued his video-game point. He was too tired and assumed that like most adults, no matter how benevolent, Moon was completely impenetrable with regard to a child's feelings or opinion. And so, Joey balanced his hatred for and also simultaneous appreciation of Moon in silence. If, somehow, one could splice Dotty's boisterousness and humor and honesty with Moon's kindness and stability and sobriety, then that, Joey thought, would be an adult he could deal with.

But he could see disappointment in his mother, too. She wasn't ready to stay sober for so long. She threw tantrums with Moon when he wouldn't let her buy things, cursing him any time she didn't get her way. And though Moon tried to please her, Joey got the sense that it was more work tending to her than to her kids. Their nightly arguments turned to daily ones, whereby eventually Keisha acquired crack, and using in Moon's house out in Croydon was out of the question. At a stalemate, Joey's mother got quiet. She was more like JuJu Man then. She lost weight and every time she got high in the house, she would pretend it never happened. Before the summer was even over, Moon was ready to quit. It was either she return to rehab, or she had to go. And she was *never goin back to nobody's fuckin rehab.*

So Joey and Mika and JuJu Man were returned to Frankford before the end of summer like dirty jewelry from a pawn shop. They had gone around the world in ninety days and lived to tell the tale. Once Popop regained ownership of the children, Keisha was gone again. And her time away grew longer with each instance. Moon, though, who broke down in tears when dropping the kids off, sent them all holiday cards for years afterward, despite the fact that he, just like the children, knew he would never really get Keisha back.

The summer before high school, Joey is the tallest Poké-mon Master at Benny's trading card store on Torresdale Ave. And he suspects he might be the only one with chest and underarm and pubic hair; he never says this out loud. It's a secret, one of those closely held inner thoughts that makes him feel like a person. It's not like he wants to brag or draw attention to himself, but he'd already seen other kids' cards, and what he's got in his right hand will elicit shock, awe, and, most importantly, victory. On his road to being a Pokémon Master, which is, of course, his destiny, he bought a single pack of cards, slicing open the plastic and pulling back the sleeve slowly. And at the back of the pack, past a bunch of grass-crawling derps like Caterpie, he finds a first-edition holographic Dragonite. His heart stops at this dream come true. Dragonite sits there on her thick orange thighs in a bright field drenched in rainbow-patterned holographic sunlight, appearing more innocent than her one hundred and twenty hit points and normal-type attack—slam, for 40X damage—might suggest. She stares into Joey's eyes, as if they were meant to be together and this is not something she is ashamed of, her left claw holding up her chin, tiny wings behind her, at rest. It is difficult for Joey to comprehend that this, the most beautiful post–middle school event of his life, is happening. No more Harding, ever. Just his new life with Dragonite.

The other children at Benny's are fascinated.

"Oh shit, man, you're so lucky," they say.

"Oh my God. Do you want to trade?!"

They offer holographic Charizards, Mewtos, Scythers, almost like they know about Joey's soft spot for praying mantises or frustrated dragons or telepathic social outcasts.

There are two other boys present who Joey will come to know. Ryan and Terrell. The former is a chubby white boy from Mayfair, the latter an older black boy with braids like A.I. albeit with much weaker hang time. They both play it cool about the Dragonite, Ryan more so than Terrell. Terrell obviously wants Joey's Dragonite, and Joey wants to learn how to be a black boy for more years and with more confidence and still be allowed to collect Pokémon cards and be alive. Even though Joey has no intention of giving the card up, he negotiates with Terrell and wants to see his deck. Only a few minutes have passed from the opening of the pack when another black boy from outside steps halfway into the store and socks Joey, snatching Dragonite out of his hand, smacking the rest of the cards on the ground.

The other kids all go wild.

"Oh my God!" they say.

"That's not right!"

"Hey!" Benny yells. "Get back here!"

But Joey says nothing. He doesn't run after them, and his surprise, mingled with confusion, lasts only a second before remembering how things really are. He stands there, waiting for something different to happen, for another choice to appear. Some kids, along with Benny, too, step out of the door to look around, but the thief is long gone. More than being bitter about the fact that, yet again, it is a black boy he is forced into conflict with, Joey is ashamed. It's is clear that Benny isn't used to having black people in his store at all, and Joey had walked quite a way to get there and feel fake safe. The man's face says that he expected something like this, too, even if it were only Joey and Terrell there. The man has the face of the social workers, the grade school teachers, the cops lingering at Margaret and Orthodox.

But eventually Joey walks outside looking up and down the street as programmed, as expected after a theft. The bandits are still long gone, the Dragonite is still long gone. But Ryan and Terrell are there, staring at him.

"That sucks," Ryan says.

"Damn, man, I'm sorry," Terrell says.

And even though he doesn't want to, Joey starts crying. Some things just never change. He knows from experience that this will only make things worse. Everyone stands and stares at him or looks away in discomfort. Joey is expecting, at this point, that sharks will smell blood in water; the laws of the wilderness will come into play, and that weak boy crying will lose not one but all of his cards to a scramble of hands, feet, and curses. Kids will grab those that fell to the ground and dig into his pockets quickly, before taking off just like that first boy. Again. But *fuck that*, he thinks. He has to stop crying. And instead, the strangest thing happens. Ryan, unable to talk about what just happened, picks up some of Joey's cards and stands near him. He doesn't laugh. He doesn't smile. He doesn't reach into Joey's pockets.

He just says it again. "Man, that really sucks. I'm sorry."

Benny, for his part, decides to give Joey a free pack of Pokémon cards, after the boy's proving that he is safe perhaps because he's such a sissy. Joey opens the pack and deflates at the garbage inside: some Zubats and Sandshrews, a Fire Energy; he fakes a closed-mouth smile, though, so as not to appear ungrateful.

Ryan, still standing next to Joey, asks if he wants to play video games at his house around the corner. And Terrell asks if he likes *Dragon Ball Z*, which by this point is a rather complicated question. Joey is elated and terrified at once. He imagines that this must just be out of pity, or that these boys are trying to trick him into more trouble. What if Ryan's house is too clean and Joey stands there trembling and afraid to touch anything? He might shrink outside of the doorway rather than sully Ryan's family property with his body. What if he has to talk to Ryan's parents, which Joey assumes correctly that he has, since the other boy lives inside a house in Mayfair?

But Ryan's parents are nothing but nice to Joey, and hardly

the fake nice he expected. They will offer him dinner every time he comes over, which he will decline every time until he doesn't. The boys will eat Tastykakes and lunch meats, play *Halo* and *Final Fantasy 11*, and watch AMVs on high-speed internet, and no one in the house will ever curse or beat them. And despite this, Joey will keep expecting the hurt that never comes. He'll spend more time at Ryan's house now than he ever will at school.

SOME SUMMERS

Feel like they'll never end. And when things are going well, even exceedingly well, let's say somebody's sister is tryna do it to you and you wanna do it with her but yall both kinda scared and you change your minds and sneak into this closed pool in the Northeast and make out all night with your clothes on and she says she loves you, but you know she doesn't really mean it and still you don't feel like she's lying, even then, on those nights, you can't help but think that something is gonna go real wrong. Even when it doesn't. Possibility exceeds reality. But it's still warm, you have that. School is out. Some summers, you'll change shape and in the following years relatives who used to fuck you up will say, *Oh he done got so big now!* And reach up to try and pat you on the head and you'll slap their fucking hands down and stare in awe at their confusion. Embarrassment slips away. Some summers you'll sneak in and out of grown women's houses and nary a real lover will catch you. You'll go out so far on your bike that you can't find the El no more and it won't even matter what time you get back cause you got a key now. You'll stay up all night on the game and in the morning, before anybody wakes up, you'll be gone and out the door to do it again.

L ate one night you find yourself returning from the movies at Franklin Mills Mall on the bus, playing *Pokémon Red* on the coolest Game Boy Color that ever existed. It's that see-through purple, you call it; and purple is now admittedly your favorite color, but you leave that fact out of most conversations, having learned better by now and anticipating all the exploitable weaknesses that something like a desire for the color purple might signify in a body like yours. You say gray, you say brown, black, red, whatever, dancing around the would-be immaterial desire for something as simple as a color. Through your Game Boy you can see all the little wires twisting around each other, gears spinning and voltage jostling it to life from two AA batteries. The innards run no less efficiently for your staring, and it feels good to finally understand what's happening.

And from the Safari Zone Sea, you fish out a Dratini, not yet a sea monster, but a little blue snake with its round mouth, more harmless than a Garter. You think, *how does it defend itself?* But you learn, battle after battle, as Dratini—

nicknamed Spike—faints over and over again to the other one hundred and fifty of its potential friends, that it can hardly defend anything, let alone its own name. You figure Spike has it bad; he's so weak. But this makes you love him more. Until one day Spike evolves, first into Dragonair, a slightly taller, darker snake who drops off its baby fat and picks up a little confidence, and then into Dragonite, the love of your life. You wonder, but only for a moment, if the affection you feel for this pocket monster is real enough to matter. You imagine your palms sliding down the scales of Dragonite's soft belly and hearing him coo in delight, feel his tiny wings on the back of your head as you lay with him in the tall grass, a whole picnic basket propped up for the two of you. But most of all, you're proud of what he's become, what you've become together: one Pokémon Master at the Elite Four's gate plus one baby snake plucked from the ocean on a cheap fishing rod, all grown up at the end game and the beginning of life.

Your friend Terrell sits across from you on the bus. He's skinny, almost as tall as you with needy braids and long, dirty nails that you sometimes clown him about. Later, you'll think that he definitely cheats with them, somehow, when shuffling and cutting the Yu-Gi-Oh! cards, but in this moment, he cannot fuck with you in Pokémon. This, you think, is because Terrell doesn't know what Dragonite is all about. He underestimates the realness under that tender pot belly, all the light he cannot see, those effort values for which no rare candy trick will suffice.

"But we're all level a hundred," he says. "How the fuck is that one so much stronger?"

You don't say that Spike has a name, but you do laugh when Spike takes down Terrell's Pokémon in four-on-one matchups, the short link cable between your two Game Boy Colors like an umbilical cord without the trouble of parents.

The back of the bus is mostly empty this time of night coming from Franklin Mills. Already, you can't remember the unremarkable film you two went to see or why Ryan isn't with you. It's an hour ride total, plenty of time to put in work on the Elite Four and your friend who cannot quite understand the consecutive Ls.

You start to think that the other Pokémon in your party are getting fed off Dragonite's labor, especially Golbat. Everybody hates Golbat. He gets no love because of the whole Zubat-in-a-cave situation, the endless loop of walking and battling and walking and battling them that you can never escape because Zubat just keeps popping up all manner of aggressive for what, from your perspective as a player, seems like absolutely no reason. But Zubat is angry and confused, maybe even lonely and sad. And there are so many Zubats, everywhere, with nowhere to go, no one to protect them. Their entire lives consist of knocking into Pokemon trainers and being slapped around by stronger Pokemon who already have homes and social resources, warm Poké Balls to sleep in. And so you feel for the Zubats and let a Golbat or two warm the bench in your party, feeding them tasty treats and sometimes letting them in on the fun of fighting.

But mostly, it's just one hyperbeam after the next, 2-D creatures screaming, squealing and being knocked off screen by the one and only Spike. Smiling at Terrell, you think, *Damn,*

I am really bussin this nigga ass right now. It's almost unfair. That you brought Dratini up from birth, though, grounds you. You are grounded. You put in work. No rare candies over here, just hard-earned hours of grinding day and night because Dragonite did not wake up like this. This is what it means to start from the bottom and finally get somewhere. Pride can't describe the buzz of intoxication. You glance over at Terrell and chuckle a little, thinking this nigga aint even ready. He aint never gonna be ready in this here *Pokémon Red.*

Outside the bus windows everything is dark. No street-lights. The bell rings for someone's stop and as the back doors open, a slightly older black boy snatches your Game Boy Color and socks you in the face.

"Pussy!" he says, hissing like a snake and running off the bus with your Game Boy.

You're not as hurt as you should be physically; he swung with the soft part of his hand, a half-open palm intending to chump you rather than knock you out. The rage bubbling up inside you is not from pain, but from an aching desire to just be left the fuck alone today.

Terrell jumps up right away. "What the fuck?" he says, looking back and forth between you and the boy darting off into the night. His face is confused about what the two of you should do, but it will definitely be something.

You're breathing a little heavier, labored, the way it always happens before you cry. But you don't cry because there's no time. Terrell has already pocketed his own Game Boy and is halfway off the bus giving chase. You follow him. Realizing the dark; you hate yourself for not looking up from the game earlier, for slacking in vigilance. You knew this could happen and you let it happen; like a child you were too busy enjoying yourself to watch for threats. This makes you angry enough to kill. You recall how much grass you had to cut for that Game Boy and you think of putting the boy who snatched it under the lawn mower face-up to the blades. This, second to Terrell being with you, is what gives you the strength to sprint out into the Roosevelt Mall parking lot.

But the boy ahead of you is quick. Turning back and seeing you and Terrell, he slams the Game Boy on the ground. Its pieces flicker apart in different directions, and you can hear the tiniest bits of plastic coming to a stop far from the impact site. Those little purple flecks could be mistaken for glass in the right light. The boy seems surprised that you and your friend are still giving chase. He must have thought smashing the Game Boy would be the end of it, that he'd walk home after a joyous victory. You don't know what you'll do, or how you'll do it when you catch him, but you damn sure don't slow down. He does. The boy comes to a stop, laughing. He seems so entertained, so happy. You curse and yell and ask questions. *What the fuck is wrong with you? Why would you do that? How could you do that?*

Your voice cracks. You are thirteen, after all. It's that time and yet, it's always that time. You feel too old to be asking the same dumb questions.

The boy is still laughing when you realize he's not alone in the dark parking lot. He has friends, too, other boys there, smoking, who must've been waiting for him. He lifts up his shirt and the silver gun in his waistband outshines the Game Boy pieces like the sun to a busted halogen bulb.

"What, pussy?" he says, grinning. He untucks it to make a point.

You understand the point now, the insides, like that time on Torresdale, at Bridge and Pratt, on Glenloch. The boy and his friends laugh and laugh, and as you cry a little, but not a lot, Terrell nudges you away, back toward the bus stop. You've missed the last one for the night, so yall walk the rest of the way home, a few hours talking shit about how grimey niggas always wanna start fights. About how only bitch niggas carry guns anyway. You talk about how yall would have beat the shit outta them if they were fair, if things were fair. Perhaps this makes you feel tougher than you should, but you've learned the importance of these performances. You poke your chest out, though you don't want to go back home and get in trouble for being sad.

Among the gripes that you and your friend Terrell have about grimey niggas, there is jealousy sprinkled in among all the hate. You are both jealous of how known and cared for these boys so often are; as you can recall it, the meanest boys you've encountered all have mommies and sometimes even daddies who care about them, hardworking parents with three and four jobs who cry on television asking that their baby simply be saved from the street while said baby is beating your ass and calling you a faggot, pistol-whipping you in the schoolyard, kicking your face into the dirt. As you and Terrell see it, these boys are spoiled children, escaping a decent life, and brutalizing, for no other reason than the budding desire to be cool and independent in a new flock or maybe avoid some fucking chores, while you and Terrell are forced to dodge their assaults and hide out in the basement of your white friend's house. Or at least that's what you tell yourself.

You are jealous because these are the boys who will have ethnographies written about them, documentaries and television programs, who are calculated as problems, and therefore, seen. You are jealous because they have the confidence to exist, albeit if only toward redemption, which they will be offered again and again, despite everything. You want to be them, but you also want to be dead. You want an alternative that isn't exceptional. You want, at this moment, for someone to pay. But you also want to be honest and acknowledge that that someone is also you, that your hatred for them is wasteful, and that they are so sad too.

As your confidence moves back into reality, you turn to Terrell, but before you can speak, he does.

"It's cool, man," he says, putting one arm around you. "You can stay at my house tonight." And even though Terrell's house also has roaches and you'll sleep on the floor, it matters so much less than the simple gesture you've been waiting for all this time. It was never Terrell's job to care for you, but it is the first time a person does and you believe them. And this is the only reason why, tonight, you don't just give up.

ACKNOWLEDGMENTS

I'm inevitably gonna miss folks, and yet. Thank you first to Dr. Aisha Lockridge, who, in addition to convincing me that we could be better and that language might change my life, let me, my kids, and my dog stay with her and hers on occasion while I drove back and forth from Notre Dame, where I was doing my MFA, to Philly, where my family was. Thank you to folks at Notre Dame who offered valuable criticisms, especially my adviser Roy Scranton. I have to thank my sister for keeping me honest while writing this and my nephew young Juju for doing more than just surviving. Thank you, Mom, for being as honest as you can. Thank you, too, to my friends, who keep me from being able to pretend: Tasia, Clarence (and that nigga who threatened us at Penn's), Bruce, Elias, Jonah, Rebecca, Tanya, TK, Nia, James, Jaquira, Maya, Muriel, Drake, Daisuke, Rebecca A., Young Cathy, and to Aaron for being the first to make me cry in a writing workshop. Thank you to the whole Spec Fic Rocketship crew. Thank you to my kids—Jojo, Leah, Max, and Elias—for being silly and child-like despite the world. Thank you, Mitch and Kiese, Hilary and Carmen. Thank you, PJ and Maddie and everyone at HBG for trusting me as an intern and an author. Thank you everybody. Thank you to tears.

READING GROUP GUIDE

DISCUSSION QUESTIONS

1. *Sink* opens with the line: "Of all the protagonists in this story—both real and imagined—just Joey, the boy, owned an Easy-Bake Oven." This is one example of the shaky borders between real and fantastical Joey's retelling of events. In what ways do moments of fantasy help or hurt Joey?

2. How would you describe Joey's self-image at the beginning of the book? How would you describe it at the end? How have his family members, friends, tormentors, and even his pets contributed to his view of himself at various stages?

3. With visceral descriptions of an apartment with roaches, but no doors, and a Philadelphia neighborhood with people, but few friends, the setting of *Sink* can be unforgiving. As outsiders, or those who grew up under different circumstances than Joey, it's easy to forget that there's joy to be found in these places as well. What are some moments in which Thomas submerges us in that joy?

4. After a brutal beating from Popop, which followed a traumatic event at Joey's school, *Sink* cuts to an interlude: "Things aren't exactly looking up for our heroes, folks... What will

they do? What will the boy do with them?... Find out next time, on *Dragon Ball Z*." The "Find Out Next Time" trope is popular with episodic TV and anime, which Joey consumes regularly. Why does Thomas introduce the interlude here? How does it affect the resolution you're anticipating to Joey's story at this point in the book?

5. How does Thomas approach the concept of childhood in *Sink*? Between Tia, Joey, Mika, and Julian, who is or isn't allowed to experience certain aspects of childhood? What is the boundary between childhood and adulthood? How might that boundary be blurred?

6. Joey is criticized for his perceived lack of manhood throughout this memoir, by none more aggressively than Popop. According to Popop's worldview, what makes a man? In what ways does Joey accept or reject these expectations of manhood?

7. The protagonist of *Sink* is male, but some of the boldest characters and voices (Tia, Erica, Dotty) are female. In the face of toxic masculinity displayed by many of the male characters (Popop, Kevin, even Joey himself), how does the author manage to express the strength and individuality of female characters?

8. Of the many characters in *Sink*, who is or isn't deserving of our sympathy? Joey, for example, is the victim of multiple acts of violence and abuse, but later confronts his own

capacity to inflict violence and abuse onto others. Does Joey's fallibility diminish our sympathy for him? What about characters like Popop, Ganny, and Keisha? To what lengths are you willing to extend your sympathies?

9. Central to Joey's understanding of himself and those around him is his understanding of Black identity and the experience of being Black in America. How does Joey understand his own Blackness, and what shapes his perception? In what ways is he forced to confront the implicit biases, microaggressions, and outright racism of the world at large?

10. After moving in with Dotty, Joey is tasked with multiple chores, one of which being the cleaning of the sink. "There was something in him, some filth that could not be scraped clean, no matter how hard and how long he might attempt excavation. The sink seemed to embody this conundrum." How does this metaphor of the sink apply to the narrative as a whole? How might it have influenced the title?

11. *Sink* takes place between the late '90s and the early 2000s. On both a small and large scale, how does that era shape and inform the story being told? In what ways is the temporal setting meaningful or meaningless?

12. Why do you think the author has chosen to end the narrative where he does? Does the book end on a sad or hopeful note? What sort of future do you envision for Joey?

ABOUT THE AUTHOR

Joseph Earl Thomas is a writer from Frankford whose work has appeared or is forthcoming in *VQR*, *N+1*, *Gulf Coast*, *The Offing*, and *The Kenyon Review*. He has an MFA in prose from the University of Notre Dame and is a doctoral candidate in English at the University of Pennsylvania. An excerpt of his memoir, *Sink*, won the 2020 Chautauqua Janus Prize and he has received fellowships from Fulbright, VONA, Tin House, and Bread Loaf. He's writing the novel *God Bless You, Otis Spunkmeyer*, and a collection of stories, *Leviathan Beach*, among other oddities. He is an associate faculty member at the Brooklyn Institute for Social Research, as well as the director of programs at Blue Stoop in Philadelphia.